T0031349

This stunning book is like being [in] (Jana's) office and listening to th[...] whose transparency is so lucid an[d ...] the feelings and hear the pulses of her heart. In *You Are Safe Now* the church is provided with one of the most important books on codependency, on spiritual abuse, on therapeutic finesse, and on a pastor who realized something was not right and was called to put an end to it. Right then and there Tricia heard, "You are safe now," and the healing began. A redemptive book of insight, grace, forgiveness, and healing.

> **SCOT McKNIGHT,** coauthor (with Laura Barringer) of *A Church Called Tov* and *Pivot*

An achingly raw and redemptive book. Tricia and Jana masterfully unveil the tactics of abusers and the realities of trauma while simultaneously showing the rescue and goodness of God. I hope that every pastor and counselor will read this book to learn how to come alongside victims—and that every person harmed by abuse can encounter the safety and hope in these pages.

> **AUBREY SAMPSON,** pastor; cohost of *The Nothing Is Wasted Podcast*; and author of *The Louder Song, Known,* and *Big Feelings Days*

You Are Safe Now reads as the work of a master storyteller paired with the professional insight of a compassionate witness and expert guide. Together, Tricia and Jana have provided a significant contribution to the literature on abuse. This is a gift to all those who seek a better understanding of the complex dynamics of interpersonal exploitation and a clear, hopeful, practical guide for the healing journey.

> **WADE MULLEN, PHD,** author of *Something's Not Right: Decoding the Hidden Tactics of Abuse and Freeing Yourself from Its Power*

You Are Safe Now is both a courageous and vulnerable memoir and a wise and kind guide. Tricia Williford's bravery in recounting her season of abuse and grief will both encourage and bring healing to the reader, while Jana Richardson's therapeutic narration will offer psychological explanations and tangible next steps. Someone in or coming out of abuse will find a pathway in *You Are Safe Now*, and someone walking alongside a healing victim will have a clearer understanding of how to show empathy and support. This is a beautiful and needed book.

ELISABETH KLEIN, coach; podcaster at *All That to Say*; and author of *Unraveling* and *World Split Open*

You Are Safe Now is one of those rare books that is as moving as it is instructional. Tricia is a gifted and talented writer, and the way she brings readers into her story and points us to hope and healing is inspirational and eye-opening. For those who want to learn how to travel from "victim" to "survivor" (or lead others on the journey), this book is a gem.

GARY THOMAS, bestselling author

I could not put this book down. I sat down to glance at the first chapter . . . and before I stood up, I had devoured it cover to cover. Tricia and Jana have done something extraordinary, unlike anything I've encountered before in books on trauma. I believe this honest journey about the life cycle of abusive patterns and relationships will not dysregulate your nervous system, will not retraumatize you. Instead, the authors' honest and kind words will wrap around you like a warm blanket, speaking in the voices of trusted friends guiding you through the hardest parts. Somehow, even though the truth telling is hard, the path toward healing and healthy intimacy becomes clear. I trust that when you emerge from these pages, you will find yourself stronger.

CATHERINE MCNIEL, author of *Fearing Bravely: Risking Love for Our Neighbors, Strangers, and Enemies*

You Are Safe Now

Safe Now

A Survivor's Guide to Listening
to Your Gut, Healing from Abuse,
and Living in Freedom

Tricia Lott Williford
with Jana Richardson, MA, LPC, EMDR

A NavPress resource published in alliance
with Tyndale House Publishers

NavPress.com

You Are Safe Now: A Survivor's Guide to Listening to Your Gut, Healing from Abuse, and Living in Freedom

Copyright © 2024 by Tricia Lott Williford with Jana Richardson. All rights reserved.

A NavPress resource published in alliance with Tyndale House Publishers

NavPress and the NavPress logo are registered trademarks of NavPress, The Navigators, Colorado Springs, CO. *Tyndale* is a registered trademark of Tyndale House Ministries. Absence of ® in connection with marks of NavPress or other parties does not indicate an absence of registration of those marks.

The Team:
David Zimmerman, Publisher; Caitlyn Carlson, Acquisitions Editor; Elizabeth Schroll, Copyeditor; Olivia Eldredge, Managing Editor; Lindsey Bergsma, Designer; Sarah K. Johnson, Proofreading Coordinator

Cover photograph of circles copyright © Evie Shaffer/Unsplash.com. All rights reserved.

Author photo copyright © 2023 by Jennie Bennett Photography. All rights reserved.

Poem "To the person named Destruction" from *Where Hope Comes From* by Nikita Gill, 2021, published by Hachette Books, reproduced by kind permission by David Higham Associates.

The author is represented by the literary agency of WordServe Literary, www.wordserveliterary.com.

Unless otherwise indicated, all Scripture quotations are taken from the *Holy Bible*, New Living Translation, copyright © 1996, 2004, 2015 by Tyndale House Foundation. Used by permission of Tyndale House Publishers, Carol Stream, Illinois 60188. All rights reserved. Scripture quotations marked NIV are taken from the Holy Bible, *New International Version,*® *NIV.*® Copyright © 1973, 1978, 1984, 2011 by Biblica, Inc.® Used by permission. All rights reserved worldwide. Scripture quotations marked TLB are taken from *The Living Bible*, copyright © 1971 by Tyndale House Foundation. Used by permission of Tyndale House Publishers, Carol Stream, Illinois 60188. All rights reserved.

This book reflects the author's present recollections of experiences over time. Some of the anecdotal illustrations in this book are true to life and are included with the permission of the persons involved. Some names and characteristics have been changed, some events have been compressed, and some dialogue has been recreated. All other illustrations are composites of real situations, and any resemblance to people living or dead is purely coincidental.

For information about special discounts for bulk purchases, please contact Tyndale House Publishers at csresponse@tyndale.com, or call 1-855-277-9400.

ISBN 978-1-64158-280-3

Printed in the United States of America

30	29	28	27	26	25	24
7	6	5	4	3	2	1

for the victims and the survivors,

for those who treat them,

and for those who love them

Contents

Important Note

This book contains sensitive themes, including emotional abuse, spiritual abuse, manipulation, sexual assault, and other violations by a person in a position of trust and spiritual authority. While the approach and structure aim to provide observational and empowering guidance and have been reviewed and edited with a trauma-informed lens, elements of the story may be triggering to survivors. We encourage gentleness with yourself. Feel the freedom to step away or to read this book in coordination with a trauma-informed therapist.

The material in this book presents an overview of the trauma of, treatment of, and recovery from an assault and abusive relationship. Every effort has been made to provide accurate and dependable information, and each chapter has been woven with discretion regarding which details to include from this individual account. This book has been compiled with clinical and legal professionals.

Change is unfolding every day regarding the patterns and treatments of abusive relationships, and the reader should be aware that professionals in this clinical field may have differing opinions. Each case and individual is different, and the material in this book is not offered as a uniform method for any single person's recovery. Therefore, the authors, contributors, publisher, and editors cannot be held responsible for any error, omission, or outdated material.

The information in this book is presented for the purposes of education and healing. Reading this book is not a substitute for receiving informed professional advice specific to an individual. Do not use this information to diagnose or treat a mental-health problem without personally consulting a licensed physician or other helping professional.

There are always more survivors than
there are therapists available.
There is always more wreckage than can be repaired.

It is amazing how little effort it takes to disrupt people's lives,
and how much it takes to put them back together.

To have your time, your body, your emotional labor,
and your altruism—especially your altruism—
stolen from you for years . . . I don't
know that that ever goes away.

The only way that gets turned into something positive is when
that person is able to really fathom the depth of it and say,
"I'm never going to let that happen to someone else."

MATTHEW REMSKI, *CONSPIRITUALITY* (PODCAST)

People forget that their actions
not only have consequences,
but victims and witnesses.

People who will carry what you said
or did within their bone marrow,
your disrespect in their sinews.

You are chaos theory:
a butterfly who caused a hurricane
for which you refuse to take responsibility.

There is no goodness in that.
Still, I hope you are safe and warm
and happy wherever you are.

NIKITA GILL, "TO THE PERSON NAMED DESTRUCTION"

This Is How It Happens

Jana

If abusers wore name tags, and if manipulators wore menacing capes and entered stage left to ominous music, then perhaps we might recognize them before they ruin people's lives.

But they do not announce their intentions before they begin, and most victims don't recognize abusers until the damage is done.

The harm caused by human perpetrators is profound, lasting, and shockingly common. We don't want to live in fear of the people around us, but we must also be alert and aware. Abuse happens all around us, and sometimes it happens *to* us. Often, the abusers live among us.

As a licensed mental-health therapist, I've seen and assessed the damage in my office time and time again. Though the voices of victims and details of harm are unique, one common denominator prevails: The victim never thought something like this could happen to them.[*]

I've worked with teachers, doctors, and other mandated reporters—people with training to know what to look for—who have been manipulated, duped, conned, or themselves abused.

I've counseled the self-proclaimed helicopter parent whose teenager was lured by a sexual predator online. Though the parent monitored screen time and screen names, kept passwords locked up and curfews locked down, the perpetrator still reached their child.

I've worked with a therapist who decided to try dating online and fell prey to a con artist who needed just a little cash to get out of a tight spot. The therapist sent money without ever meeting this person, and now he's a target of identity fraud and debt collections that are swallowing him whole.

I've treated the nurse who works with victims of sexual assault and does the rape kits, and who unknowingly picked up a drink spiked with a date drug, waking up to the same harm and trauma her patients had experienced.

I've seen the damage of more covert abuse as well, such as the aftermath of a controlling parent or a verbally abusive supervisor in the workplace. This kind of abuse can cause damage to a person's psyche that may take decades to recover from.

---

[*] To protect the privacy and anonymity of my clients, the following illustrations are composites of real situations.

I've seen terrible things happen to smart people. And when I say "smart people," I am referring to intelligence of every kind—book smart, street smart, multiple degrees, leadership skills, high emotional intelligence.

In this book, we are telling the story of an abusive relationship between a church leader and a person in the congregation, so let's look at what we know about this particular dynamic. Abuse in a spiritual context has layers of harm, but in every case there is a built-in power imbalance: The leader's influence cannot be separated from their spiritual practice, which means they implicitly and falsely apply God's voice, approval, and credibility to their words and actions, no matter how harmful.

The scope of this problem isn't easy to identify or discuss. Hard data and accurate statistics, particularly anything that gives a sense of the extent of abuse in faith context,[1] are difficult to find. Based on what we do know, the research doesn't include what is certainly the majority of abuse. The limited information we do have, however, is still deeply troubling:

- "Clergy sexual misconduct with adults is . . . prevalent across all denominations, all religions, all faith groups, all across the country."[2] While Catholic churches have been the subject of most media attention, the problem is also great with Protestant churches.[3]

- "In the average American congregation of 400 persons, with women representing, on average, 60% of the congregation, there are [an] average of 7 women who have experienced clergy sexual misconduct."[4]

- Further, "92% of these sexual advances [reported by women as sexual misconduct by clergy toward themselves] had been made in secret, not in open dating relationships; and 67% of the offenders were married to someone else at the time of the advance."[5]

- Data reveals specific location types of clergy sexual abuse, including at the church, in the offender's home, and at the victim's home.[6]

- "You are more likely to be abused by someone in the church, than your congregation being involved in a shooting."[7]

While these statistics can be unsettling and hard to believe, they cannot be ignored. Abusers are not tucked away in the margins of society, and the occurrences of abuse are not limited to any small portion of our communities.

I have counseled victims of abusers in schools, on sports teams, and in community groups. I've seen people who've been targeted by their employers, coaches, helpers in the classroom, and close friends. And, tragically, as the statistics show, not even our churches are a refuge from those who would harm their fellow human beings. I've worked with traumatized victims of senior pastors, youth pastors, volunteers—men and women alike. These patterns have reached pandemic levels even in—sometimes especially in—our churches.

We prefer to think we are exempt from manipulation and abuse because of our choices, our age, our education, our life experience. We want to think we are protected because we know the red flags to watch for. But evil and sin do not discriminate. The brokenness of our fellow human beings exists in every part of our world. We want to believe we are smart enough to stay safe, to keep our people safe. When terrible things have been done to us, we tend to feel shame and, wrongly, responsibility.

Hear me on this:

If you have experienced harm at the hands of another person, *it is not your fault.*

You didn't need to be smarter or better or more careful.

When abuse occurs, it is the perpetrator's fault.

It is never the fault of the victim.

Abuse is about power and control, and for someone who is broken enough to harm another human being, power and control must be maintained at all costs. So this person skirts the edges of the law, hurting people in noncriminal ways that we widely regard as unethical, dishonest, irresponsible, and in violation of what is socially appropriate. Not all predators are operating in crime circles of the upper-echelon elite in big cities. They haven't all been convicted, and many of them haven't been found out. Some of them live in your neighborhood, some of them work in your building, and some of them are standing in front of the congregation on Sunday mornings.

Abuse exists on a broad spectrum, and further, abusers exist on a spectrum of their own awareness. At one end, we see manipulators who can be stunningly oblivious to the damage of their own patterns. If they have grown up in systems saturated with manipulation, it can become the only way they know how to relate to others. Along the middle of the spectrum are emotional and verbal abusers who may or may not hurt people on purpose. Sometimes they say things without thinking, and other times their actions are cunning and direct. And at the far opposite end, we see sociopaths, abusive narcissists, and predators who target individuals and groups of people both masterfully and intentionally. Habitual abusers can be skilled at acting in ways that allow them to continue to abuse without experiencing the consequences of their behavior. Some of them have learned how to rewrite reality—even for themselves—to justify their behavior, to center themselves as the one in the right.

Predators can be virtuosos in the art of manipulation. They watch carefully, and they make calculated choices. They know how to groom, taking small steps and careful measures toward their end goal. By the time a predator has targeted you, they may know you better than you know yourself. Anyone can be targeted by a predator, and even experts can fall prey. Robert Hare, a professor emeritus of psychology at the University of British Columbia, writes that they "can play a concerto on *anyone's* heartstrings."[8] Anyone can become at risk.

When I met Tricia, her husband had died just weeks before. She was exhausted and depleted, and she nearly crumpled into the chair in my office. She was grieving a horrific loss, yes. But even from the start, I sensed that something else was going on. There was an injured soul trapped inside her, wounded by more traumas than the one she'd presented.

Many people know Tricia's story. The loss of her husband was fairly high-profile in our community, and her writing has carried her story around the world. But very few people know the complex nature of her wounding, which included a second trauma that happened alongside the death of her husband. Tricia and I have invested more than twelve years of weekly sessions together, untangling the complexities of what happened to her.

I have partnered with Tricia to tell this story because we believe in the power of knowledge and experience to set people free. As she writes about the trauma she walked through, I am writing about her treatment. She shares the candid memories of a trusted friendship twisted horribly wrong, and I pull back the curtain to show you the textbook patterns that were present all along: of predation, grooming, psychological manipulation, and abuse. While the details of this story come from a unique situation, the pattern of it is universal. You may not have this experience, but you may have an experience that parallels this one.

We write this book because our best defense against abuse is understanding the nature of abusers. Our best path to freedom is being able to see and name what we're experiencing. The ability to see and know what's going on is the first step to getting help.

This book will give you a real example of what abusive patterns look like. You're going to learn to understand and identify the signs of trauma, and together we're going to walk through the journey out of abuse and into healing. The harm you or someone you love has experienced is not the end.

If you are reading this as a counselor or therapist, this book puts the language and tools of our trade alongside the lived experience of a survivor of abuse. We believe it can be a resource for you as you come alongside your clients, since our stories sometimes become clear only when we see them mirrored in someone else's life.

Some people will read this story and realize that they are victims as well. They will find words for the first time as they discover that what happened to them was systematic and wrong. And, perhaps, they will also find hope: that what has happened to them is not the end of their story. We invite you into the pages to show you how it happens, what it might look like, and how you can find freedom and recovery if you are someone—or if you are treating someone, or if you love someone—who is the survivor of abuse.

I will never not be awed by the healing process of another person. Truly, the sacredness of walking with a person through trauma, helping them heal, explore, and grow—this is an honor beyond words. It is holy and precious, and I approach each path gently and with deepest respect.

There are times when I think, *Really, God? Are you sure you want me to be the one to navigate this path? Because this is a lot.*

And then I take a deep breath, and I pray, *Okay. Then may I help them find the words and tools to reclaim what was taken. And God, may you heal what has been broken.*

I pray the same for you as you begin this book.

Together may we find the words and tools to reclaim what was taken. And may God heal what has been broken.

ONE

The Hook

Tricia

One of my college professors once told me that she didn't trust anyone who trusted their intuition. She said such illogical feelings and emotions can usually be traced back to a bad slice of pizza from the night before.

Her opinion didn't convince me that intuition isn't real. It only made me wonder what compass needle she trusted.

I know the difference between indigestion and intuition. Nausea from indigestion starts in my stomach. Nausea from intuition starts in the hair follicles of my skull.

Heightened intuition isn't always about something going wrong, but there is a specific kind of intuition for danger.

For me, it feels like the turning of dials within my nervous system, like the opening scene in the first *Back to the Future* movie, when Marty McFly is adjusting the amplifier for his surprisingly small guitar.[1] It might begin with an invisible emotional shift in the environment, a glance or an imperceptible exchange that somehow seems to affect my body temperature. I feel a tightening in my chest, then a sinking in my gut, then a racing in my pulse—loud, louder, loudest—until I absolutely cannot ignore this physiological response.

People who know me well have long joked about The Feeling, this Code Blue phrase that has always meant *Welp, hope you had fun while it lasted, because it's all about to end. Tricia is about to shut things down.*

This inner compass hasn't always been my favorite thing about myself. There have definitely been some false alarms, when I have walked away from some lit fuses that weren't actual bombs. But if I smell smoke, it's a nonstarter for me. If I sense that things are about to go sideways, I will flee the situation, the scene, the relationship—all of it. I'll scoop up my feelings and my family. Peace out.

I am telling you this because it's important to clarify: I did not get The Feeling when I first met Annie. It's important to me—and to the patterns of a story like this one—that I introduce her as the good person I thought she was.

I will give you only some basic details about Annie because you don't need to know everything about her to understand how what I went through with her followed the textbook pattern of abuse, and because—I will always be honest with you—it's risky for a victim to start talking about their abuser.

Here's what I can tell you. Annie was a Christian. She was highly intelligent and focused on community, and she had a position of spiritual authority. I had only known her from a distance for a while, the way you might know somebody who walks their dog in your neighborhood. Your paths cross, you make eye contact and smile, and you might even feel like you could become friends since it's obvious that they like the things you like—dogs and sunshine.

Annie led Bible studies, and they were refreshingly different from others I had attended. In a word, they weren't "pink." I have nothing against the actual color, mind you. But if the time together focuses on superficial small talk, recipes, perhaps "a spring fashion show" or "a Ladies' Tea"—it *feels* pink. It's the women's-ministry version of that outdated and inaccurate marketing cliché: If you want to sell your product to women, you simply "shrink it and pink it."[2] As though women will only enjoy the smaller, pastel versions of anything real. That's not true of this woman, and it's not true of most women I know.

These Bible studies were filled with dialogue; questions; and conversations about real life, messy people, and complex theology. Annie brought us into the words and ideas of theologians and scholars, making our conversations fertile ground for public learning. So many books, so many theories, so many thinkers, and so many of them with so many letters after their names.

Now seems like a good time to tell you that I am an excellent notetaker. It started when I was elected as "secretary" of various clubs in high school, mostly for my good handwriting, colorful notebooks, and endless enthusiasm for pens. Just like my pen collection, my notetaking skills grew with time. I've taken minutes at staff meetings and cataloged the content of committees. I was a professor's assistant in college and took copious notes in lectures. If you've always wondered what you missed in a random English course or literature class in the late 1990s and early 2000s, feel free to check in with me. I've probably got you covered.

At Annie's Bible studies, I took notes like it was my job. It's possible some of the women in this room weren't as intrigued as I was. They had places to be, people to talk to, ideas to execute. But in that season of my life, I had none of those things.

I had two captivating little children at home, so my long days were filled with small things[3]: emptying the dishwasher again, reading board books again, going to the park again, folding laundry again. I so badly wanted to go back to school—but sometimes you get to do exactly what you dream, and sometimes you do what keeps the family system from flying off the rails. It was my season to stay home, to create routines and structure for two toddlers. My big ideas were on hold, and I reminded myself often: It's just a pause. It's no *for now*, not no *forever*.

But as someone who gets high on smart conversations, I walked into that first Bible study like an intern at a White House briefing. My own excitement embarrassed me. I couldn't help it. I was a fish out of water. Or more accurately, I was a fish who had caught sight of the water. The deep blue was out there, and people were casually living in it, tossing around their splashy ideas. I wanted in.

Then Annie, from her seat of influence in the room, did something I've never forgotten.

"Tricia," she said. I looked up, my pen poised in midair, ready to capture her next words. I probably looked like an eager cocker spaniel waiting for a trick command and a treat for obeying.

She said, "I want to know what you think."

All eyes in the room turned to me. They weren't looking at my notes or my handwriting, my tabs or my filing systems. They were looking at me, waiting to hear my thoughts, because Annie had opened the door for me to speak. Surprising even myself, I didn't need even a moment to gather my thoughts.

I don't remember what I said. I just remember feeling heard.

The conversation stilled for just a moment, and then they all began to talk, to react, to interact with what *I* thought. From across the room, Annie gave me a thumbs-up. Her small gesture seemed to say she had seen a glimpse into my mind, and my thoughts had not disappointed.

All my relational roads lead back to conversation. Every single one. Thinking with someone is where every friendship starts for me. If you lead with a real conversation, I'll be your friend forever.

In the world of addiction, *gateway drug* is the catchphrase used to describe the probability of one drug experience leading to another, of something comparatively harmless opening the door to harder drugs that perpetuate greater dependency.

Conversation with Annie became a gateway drug. She had tapped a vein.

Jana

If you do a quick search on your TV channels or podcasting apps, you'll find dozens of documentaries and human stories combining elements of psychological warfare, true crime, and the mysteries of social history. As a society, we are binge-ing on this content as if our lives depend on it. Why are we so drawn in? Why are *so many of us* drawn in?

It seems that cults and circles of social control tend to swell during times of uncertainty,[4] and this may be one factor to explain why the public appetite seems so insatiable for these stories.

During the throes of the coronavirus pandemic, when the world was shut down and quarantined, one podcaster reported her own shock to discover that she had invested more than twenty-three hours of her life to watching long-form shows about people who had fallen deep into manipulative relationships that wrecked their lives.[5] She's not alone. Lots of us are watching.

I think what separates these shows from, say, baking competitions are our polarized responses. We might watch or listen and find ourselves thinking, *How can someone get so confused? Why would they throw their lives away for such a corrupt leader?* But then the plot twists, and we think, *I do sort of see the appeal, though. Imagine that beautiful sense of belonging.*

After the next commercial break, we come to our senses and think *Can't they see that this person is a cult leader?* But give it just a few minutes. Soon we feel compassion again as we see the draw to live in a close community with people who share values and spiritual practices.

Our own pendulums swing back and forth. As we learn their stories, we judge them and then we understand them. We question their discernment, then we see how they got duped.

If you look at someone's choice without looking at anything else about them, you might wonder how a person could make a decision like that. How could they be so deceived? How could they become so addicted? How could they break that law? But if you consider the context of the person's whole story—their season of life, their ambitions to succeed, their desperation to numb and medicate—then behaviors and choices can start to make sense.

In the clinical world of therapy, counseling, and psychology, most behaviors make sense within context. With a little empathy, we can at least imagine how they got there.

Consider the desperation of thirst. When a woman is in labor with a baby, think about how thirsty she becomes from all her exertion. She wants water *so badly*. She'll down the whole glass because she's so very thirsty. (Speaking from experience, with the birth of my son. I tried to sip. I promise, I tried.) Wise and experienced nurses know that the woman in labor doesn't have the awareness to limit herself to sips of water, so they might give her a popsicle, likely some ice chips. They allow a slow intake of fluids that won't induce immediate vomiting. It's the best way to help a thirsty person because their thirst is almost desperate.

Abusers typically prey on people who are isolated from their communities, separated from paths and social circles they once knew. These include college students; young professionals; older adults who live alone; and many young moms who feel isolated from their careers, goals, and social circles as they raise little children. Tricia felt starved for intellectual stimulation, communication, and every kind of community. Annie spotted that, and she fed it. Tricia was in a desert; Annie offered the water.

The emotional drive of ambition can feel similar to physical desperation. When physical desperation and emotional needs jive, it's a magic spell. A perfect storm. A match and a bomb. A shiny lure on a fishhook. Appropriately, an abuser's initial offer to meet that felt need has been called "the hook."[6]

The hook is a key part of a perpetrator's pattern of choosing their target, biding their time, and taking small steps to execute their goal. Even if they would say they didn't have a plan from the beginning, we can observe patterns that have happened before. Their behavior is often premeditated, calculated, serial, manipulative, and habitual. Their patterns have become their norm, but they may not want to look at it that way, so they lie to themselves and everyone else. Still, even if not every piece was intentional, if some pieces fell into place by accident or as a bonus, this is a habit the perpetrator has created, has counted on, and returns to. They are accountable for what they've done.

During the #MeToo movement, when a lot of predation patterns came to light, we learned about actresses who had been sexually assaulted and abused by television and movie producers. These producers were predators who knew what they were doing: They made casting decisions while they held the women's careers in their hands.

We learned about Larry Nassar, the doctor of the US women's Olympics gymnastics team. He was a predator who knew what he was doing, systematically sexually abusing many of the women in his care while he held their futures in his hands.

We have also learned about men and women who endure abuse in their homes and the workplace, who silence their intuition and go along with their abusers' behavior because these people project power, instill fear, or seem to hold the future in their hands. Sometimes we go along with systemic problems because it's the way things have always been: It is literally the system in place.

One podcaster discusses this common denominator: "If you're ambitious, and you want your career to go a certain direction, it actually makes you vulnerable to predation."[7]

Victims are not necessarily weak, passive, or down on their luck. Often, they are ambitious.

They are not just trying to scrape together some choices. They are driven to become the best version of themselves, to change their lives and the world. And they have been fed the lie that the only way to get ahead is to take the hit.

When we consider what we think we know about vulnerability and victims, most of us would not associate these words with ambition. But people become vulnerable because they don't realize how much they are willing to ignore, how many warning signs they are willing to push away so they can stay on the path of their goals and ideals.

An abuser can spot a weakness.

A skilled abuser can get their prey to silence their own priorities, their goals, and even their instincts.

A masterful manipulator can place themselves on the path to the goal.

TWO

Charisma

Tricia

Annie seemed to have a life straight out of an episode of *Friends*: unlocked doors, nightly meals at her big dining room table, a growing collection of catchphrases and inside jokes.

There were four or five women who were especially comfortable at Annie's house, arriving early and staying late. They helped themselves to her food, changed clothes in her bedroom. They stayed late when they hung out, watching TV together under shared blankets on the couch. They left toothbrushes at her house, tucked into her medicine cabinet. Sometimes they stayed the night all together in one grown-up sleepover, and other times one woman at a time, especially when Annie's husband was away for the evening and she didn't want to be in bed alone. These women nearly lived in Annie's home, right there along with Annie and her husband, like they'd been woven into the fabric of Annie's family.

I had never seen anything like this boundaryless place where everyone belonged to one another. Their banter and friendship reminded me of my college roommates, of the great merge of wardrobes and pantries, but this was different from dorm life. These women each had their own apartments, houses, husbands, and children to go home to, wake up to, and care for the next day. And yet they spent their evenings here, night after night, drinking wine or coffee at Annie's house.

Within a few visits to her home, Annie gave me a nickname. She said she did this with all her closest friends. It's how you knew when you were in, she told me—when she gave you a name that nobody else had, a name you had never been called.

This is, as researcher and advocate Wade Mullen identifies, a common approach among abusive people: They dismantle their victim's internal world, beginning with the victim's identity. He writes in his stunningly helpful book *Something's Not Right: Decoding the Hidden Tactics of Abuse and Freeing Yourself from Its Power*,

> Something as seemingly innocent as giving you a
> nickname is a prime example of this kind of attack,
> a form of control that replaces your given name
> with a name chosen by the abuser. . . . It may seem

harmless, but in truth, given names are important anchors to our sense of identity. Of course, those who honor your identity can, at times, use nicknames in a harmless and endearing way. However, exchanging that name with another without honoring your agency can be demoralizing, an act that strips you of the identity captured in your chosen name.[1]

I hadn't asked for a nickname, but I got a nickname nonetheless. And with it came a subtle shift in identity and belonging. I found myself answering to something I'd never been called before.

Annie did friendship in a radically different way, and her community was magnetic. The women in her circle were checking in all the time, following her around town, making appointments or dropping in for her time and attention. Annie defined it as "intentional community," this open-door, open-bed way of life. She had an entire philosophy to explain it, and Scripture to support it.

When Annie talked about her visions for what community could be, she often mentioned the description of the early church in the second chapter of Acts: They were people who "met together in one place and shared everything they had" (verse 44). She'd explain this to me over a meal at her house.

"Everything they had," she said to me, piercing my bite of chicken with her fork, putting the food in her mouth, and then trading my glass of water for her glass of wine. "Imagine what that could be like."

She invited me to stay late, but I declined the invitation

and headed home to my family. Mornings come early when you have little children, but also, I liked sleeping next to my husband. I knew he'd never be on board with the nonsense of me spending the night at another lady's house just because she wanted someone to sleep next to her. And I felt like that was one of the perks of being married: sleeping and waking up next to the same person, for as long as we both shall live.

Annie scoffed at this decision. When I look back on those conversations, I can see the subtlety in it now, the casual implications that my limits were inferior to her holier way of living in community. Soon she gave me another nickname: The Boundary Queen. My rigid boundaries reigned supreme, she teased.

Yes, it felt uncomfortable, but it also felt magical to be included in Annie's circle. Annie was incredibly charismatic and amazingly talented, the kind of person everyone wanted to be friends with. We were drawn to her like moths to a flame. I couldn't identify it then—but I know now: We had all mistaken gifts for grace.[2]

Tim Keller has taught about this tendency among the followers of gifted leaders. He has pointed out our tendency to concentrate not on the character of the leader but on the talent. When a leader is charismatic, we tend to look more at what they do than who they are.

We tend to see their spiritual gifts (preaching, teaching, administration, leadership, and other talents) as equivalent to spiritual grace, the fruit of the Spirit (love, joy, peace, patience, kindness, goodness, faithfulness, gentleness, and self-control).

As Keller says, "Gifts of the Spirit are what you do. The grace of the Spirit is who you are."[3]

Hard experience has taught me that it's dangerous to mistake someone's gifts and talents for spiritual fruit. If you raise questions about the fruit and get answers about the talents, be watchful. And when you know something isn't right yet a person tries to convince you that you're incorrect, imagining it, or crazy—that is evil at work.

I should have known. I should have seen it. I should have trusted myself. But I trusted her instead.

Jana

Con man comes from the phrase *confidence man*.[4] The original "confidence man" was dressed to the nines, from his top hat to his shoes. And while he was attractive to the eye, he was also personally engaging with those he approached. He would strike up a conversation with an unsuspecting stranger, and he would ask, "Sir, have you the confidence in me to lend me your watch, and I'll return it to you tomorrow?"

Notice the word choice: "Have you the confidence in me?"

The question he raises is not whether he can be trusted, but whether the targeted person has confidence in him. The question asks whether people consider themselves too jaded to say yes to someone who seems so pleasant, even if it's someone they've just met. Most people do not want to think themselves jaded, cynical, or untrusting, so we tamp down our uneasiness and decide to place our trust in the person who has asked for our confidence.

Charisma is the mysterious "it" factor that invites our confidence, the compelling charm that inspires us to follow business leaders, motivational speakers, YouTube sensations, and celebrity pastors. The jury is out on whether the skills of charismatic people can be learned or cultivated, but either way, this verdict is in: As a society, we are drawn to people with charisma. We cannot help ourselves.

When one person is enamored, a charismatic leader is born. When more than one person feels the same way, a charismatic group may begin to take shape. Social control often begins with a small circle of influence—and with time, space, and power, the whole thing multiplies.

Charisma on its own isn't a bad thing. Being charismatic doesn't equal being manipulative. A charismatic leader may have power over people, but that doesn't mean they abuse that power. Not every leader is corrupt. But some of them are. It is the corrupt charismatic leader who has a dark side, who uses their power to manipulate others in ways that are self-serving and destructive.

Again, it would be helpful if these manipulators wore name tags. But they don't, and they don't appear to be insane, dark, or menacing. They don't even foam at the mouth.

Charisma, after all, draws us in. A corrupt charismatic person looks like us. Has a life like ours. Is someone we want to be friends with. More than that, though, a corrupt manipulator possesses a magnetism, a way of making people feel like they belong, like they're extraordinary—especially because they have been noticed by the most extraordinary person with the power to bestow the attention.

Annie was the charismatic leader of a group of devoted followers, a circle of women who were captivated by her. She had set her sights on Tricia as her next target.

Perhaps you are wondering, *What is the difference between what we're describing and a normal, healthy friendship?* An abusive dynamic contains a power imbalance in a relationship between two people and a purposeful manipulation where only one person knows the end goal. A power imbalance exists when one person has inherently greater power than another, whether through formal hierarchy or informal influence they possess. The stronger person is the predator, and they use their influence to gain control over the subservient person through overt or subtle forms of persuasion over time. This power imbalance can exist in a marriage or domestic partnership, a boss-employee relationship, pastor-parishioner interactions, and therapist-client settings. It can happen with a professor, instructor, or mentor. Power imbalances can occur in fraternities, sororities, schools, spiritual environments—anywhere where a person might have influence and be able to use that influence to control and take advantage of another person. And because of the nature of Annie's role of spiritual authority, a power imbalance was built into Tricia's connection to Annie.

Psychologist and professor Martha Stout writes,

I have asked countless former victims whether they had any early suspicions that they were being deceived, and nearly all have given the same answer. In the beginning, they saw someone who had a great deal of charm and an intense interest in what other people had to say, someone who was very complimentary. They saw no red flags. They were without a clue until they began to be victimized, and many remained so long after that.[5]

Social abusers will charm and manipulate their way through life, leaving behind them a trail of broken hearts, shattered expectations, and stolen ambitions. Sometimes they lack conscience and feeling for others and take what they want and do as they please without the slightest sense of culpability or remorse. Other times, they're acting out of their own trauma and wounding in ways they are unable or unwilling to understand or acknowledge.

Whatever their internal motivation, acknowledged or unacknowledged, an abuser moves quickly, creating a façade of connection at the beginning of a relationship through extravagant affection. The abuser may shower the other person with gifts, compliments, flattery, constant contact, and increasing amounts of time together. They may give praise, additional attention, endless text messages, and notes of encouragement. This deceptive kind of evil can create an alluring path with words, excessive thoughtfulness, and likely the most generous friendship you've ever seen.

The abusive person will likely show you something pleasant about yourself, but this is not for the sake of your encouragement. Their motive is rooted in wanting you to think more highly of *them*, to fall in love with the way *they* make you feel, to want more time with *them*. It's a manipulative approach called love bombing,[6] and love bombing works because it's filled with a thousand truths twisted into weapons. The truth is that you are worthy of love. You are worthy of good things. You have much to offer the world. But love bombing manipulates all that truth to soften your instincts and purchase your confidence.

When someone compliments us, we want to believe their words are true. We want to believe in their confidence in us, so we put our confidence in them. They seem kind, accepting, and able to see the best version of us, so the deception becomes extremely difficult to detect. Why? Because this same encouraging dynamic exists at the beginning of a healthy, loving relationship. We cannot sniff out the difference.

This is why wisdom whispers, *Slow down*. You know the axiom "Only fools rush in"? The intimacy of friends happens over time, through shared experiences. Real relationships take time to develop. If this intimacy happens too quickly, be suspicious.

A victim will often recall feeling very, very close to the other person at the beginning, more quickly than the natural development of any other relationship. Even if you wouldn't normally bare your soul to someone you just met, an abusive person will dismantle your defenses and rush you to a place of vulnerability. A true friendship doesn't require you to expose all your vulnerabilities to someone who hasn't earned that trust, and it certainly doesn't demand that all your time and energy should focus on that person alone.

Forced intimacy is not often a sign of a lasting friendship, and it's rarely an indication that you can trust someone. Knowing whom you're in company with makes all the difference in the world.

But abusers are skilled deceivers, often even to themselves, and we get involved in something we think is healthy or beneficial or even trustworthy. An abusive person often influences us to spend more time with them and increasingly less time with friends and family, gaining the upper hand and becoming one of the primary voices we listen to. We're getting tangled in lies because we don't even know they're lying to us. We don't know how to get out because we don't know how we got in. There's a subtle power differential building. Every action has a string attached, and the abuser is spinning a tight and dangerous web.

Let's talk about the word *thrall*. It's an odd word, one we almost never hear used in a sentence. *Merriam-Webster* defines *thrall* as a noun, "a state of complete absorption."[7] This word can express the most mystical sense of rapture and delight, the twitterpation we see when one person is consumed with delight by another person.

You've likely seen *thrall* with a prefix and a suffix: the word *enthralled*. When someone is enthralled, they may feel like they've never known a friend like this, never met someone who thinks like this, never met someone who seems to know them so well.

That's exactly what an abuser wants someone to think and feel. *Enthralled* is the goal.

Thrall has another meaning: "a person in moral or mental servitude."[8] To enthrall means "to hold spellbound: charm," "to hold in or reduce to slavery."[9] I studied the work of cult expert Janja Lalich, who specializes in coercive control and relationships of undue influence, and she has pointed out this essential distinction.[10] Lalich taught me that when the charm of thralldom is combined with dishonesty, manipulation, or other mistreatment, it becomes traumatic, embarrassing, and crushing.

We don't want to believe that this could happen to us or to someone we love, but the human mind is more fragile than we would like to believe. We are all subject to influence techniques. We place our confidence in people who intended to take it from us all along.

My experience matches that of Wade Mullen: Not every kind person will become abusive or harmful to others. But nearly every person who later shows themselves to be abusive or harmful to others begins their manipulation by being exceedingly kind.[11]

By the way, by the time the original "confidence man" was convicted, he was found to be in possession of dozens of fine watches that he had never returned.

He had never intended to.

THREE

Manipulation

Tricia

At the height of our friendship, Annie and I were exchanging more than 14,000 texts a month. That's more than 450 texts a day, which is approximately 28 texts an hour, every hour, if we optimistically assume I slept for eight hours a night. Annie and I were exchanging approximately one text every two minutes. The communication was constant.

It didn't begin as an onslaught of communication. It started slowly. One evening after Bible study, she texted me to say thank you—for a great evening, for great conversation, for the start of a great thing.

When I woke up the next morning, there was another text to start the day. Her words were sprinkled with Bible verses: "Hey, good morning. I was reading this morning in Isaiah, where God said, 'Behold, I am doing a new thing.' I am excited to know you, to see what God is doing in your life, in my life, and in our friendship together."

If I didn't answer right away, she'd wait a little while and then text again to see how I was, where I was, what I was doing with my day, what I was thinking about, how she might pray for me, encourage, or help. She sent quotes and verses and thoughts from her reading. She sent messages like "This made me think of you."

"It's God's will that we met."

"You understand me more than anyone."

"I've never met anyone like you."

"Every good and perfect gift is from God. I'm thankful for the perfect gift of you."

"You are the most creative person I have ever met."

"You are the smartest woman in the room."

"You are anointed."

"You are gifted beyond measure. I am excited to see what God is doing in you."

If it sounds like endless compliments and constant attention, it was. And like a puppet, I stayed on her string. Soon, my days began and ended with her words. She texted me before my husband could say good morning, and she often sent me one more message after my husband kissed me good night. I acquired the thumb dexterity of a twelve-year-old girl, texting dozens of times a day.

She ran helpful errands, and she paid close attention to details. When she went grocery shopping for her family, she picked up a few peaches for me and dropped them off at my house. And, while she was at it, she happened to have a book in the car that someone had mentioned in our discussions the night before, a title she noticed I had written down. She was happy to lend it for as long as I'd like.

She gave intense, intentional gifts. For my birthday, she gave me a hand-thrown clay vase—baked, glazed, and painted in shades of chocolate brown and grass green. She presented it at my birthday party, a grand gesture of extravagant creativity.

When my grandmother died, she asked if she could swing by my house before I left for the airport. She had made a CD for me to listen to while I was out of town for the funeral, to guide my thoughts while I was remembering my grandma and grieving with my family. The playlist took me through the journey of nine songs, each shifting my emotions a little at a time, from lament to grief, then to heartache and sadness, then to honesty and truth, then to hope and celebration of her life.

She delivered it with a note she had made on personalized stationery decorated with Scripture—pages torn from a Bible. I remember wondering, *Who tears a page out of a Bible to decoupage onto a handwritten note? Does she have a spare Bible that she uses for arts and crafts?* It was beautiful, with an underlying message that feels darker in retrospect: When she loved someone, she was willing to ruin the sacred to display that love.

When I came back from that trip, she had bought clothes for me. She said she had noticed maybe I had lost a few pounds, that my pants seemed too big and maybe these would fit better. She also suggested maybe it was time for a wardrobe upgrade in general, that maybe I could dress a little younger, "perhaps a little more like a free-thinking adult rather than the modest product of evangelical and purity subculture." Somehow she knew my measurements, and she could buy clothes off the rack that fit me better than anything in my closet.

She said that she wanted to be my best friend. That she wanted me to feel seen and known, and she wanted to pursue the goal of knowing me better than anyone else knew me in my life. If friendships are concentric circles on a target, Annie moved into the bull's-eye. She took center stage, ultimately pushing others out, replacing them with her time and attention, her gifts and extravagance. Our lives became more and more intertwined. Afternoons together, family dinners together, couples' camping trips together. Our husbands enjoyed each other, and everybody had somebody when we served alongside each other. She was proving to me the doctrine of community: This was a holy version of the church in action.

Like another moth to the flame, I was irresistibly drawn into Annie's circle. I became one of those elite women who arrived early and stayed late to the hangouts at her house, though I still didn't feel the need to spend the night in her bed, and I didn't succumb to leaving a toothbrush.

Not until years later.

This is how life could be, she said, this level of life together.

It was easy to let her in because she seemed like one of the most intentional people I had ever known.

I wasn't wrong; she was intentional. I just didn't know her intent.

"Can I pour you a cup of coffee?" Annie asked me as I sat on a stool at her kitchen counter bar.

"No, thanks," I said. "I don't drink coffee."

She side-eyed me, like I had said I don't believe in equality for women. "Who doesn't drink *coffee*?"

"I don't."

I felt a low-grade embarrassment that was becoming familiar around Annie. How could I not like the most basic drink that seems to be the heart fuel of so many social gatherings?

"Well, I bet that's because nobody ever made the right kind for you," she said.

"How many kinds can there be? At a coffee shop I can find something on the menu, but when I'm at home, I can't figure out why or how to make a pot of something I don't like."

She opened her cupboard to display all the charms of a full coffee bar. Her eyes gleamed. She was a street-corner vendor revealing a coat full of watches.

"That's quite a selection," I said.

"I think you would like it the way I make it," she said. "Haven't you ever wished you liked coffee? Wished you could 'sip coffee with the grown-ups' after dinner?"

Oddly, yes. Especially that reference to feeling like an adult. I had secretly always liked the way the mug feels in my hand, the way people look sophisticated when they drink coffee, how the perfect mug is so great for gesturing in conversation. I envied this so much that I had long before discovered a trick: If you fill a mug with Diet Pepsi, nobody knows the difference. The key is in the slow sip. You have to pretend like it could burn you if you drink too fast.

"Here, I'll make a cup for you. What do you have to lose anyway? It's my coffee, my creamer, and if you don't like it, you can change your mind. But I do think you'll like it. Specifically, I think you'll like it *the way I make it.*"

"Sure," I allowed. "I'll try it. But seriously, I have never tasted a flavor of coffee that I've liked. So please don't be offended if I don't like it."

"Please," she said. "I am unoffendable. And if you don't like it, we will try it a different way. It's definitely an acquired taste, and you may have to taste it a few times before you start to enjoy it. That's totally normal. You go ahead and choose your mug, and look in the refrigerator for which creamer you'd like."

I chose a mug that felt right to me, and I chose a flavor that I had seen somewhere else, something I recognized as popular enough to not be terrible. I watched her make the coffee with a French press. Precise, exquisite, elegant, and European. She had done this before.

I made conversation in the concentrated silence. "Have you ever noticed that *acquired* is only used to talk about a sense of taste? Nobody ever talks about an 'acquired smell.'

Nobody ever says, 'I didn't like it at first, but I kept smelling it until I liked it.'"

She laughed. "Fair enough. I think there are probably a lot of things in the world that we can convince ourselves to like, if we keep trying them."

She stirred the coffee with a spoon, and then she licked the spoon to sample her work. She offered that same spoon to me, like this is what everyone does when someone pours them a cup of coffee. Her eyes said of course I would know that gesture if I had only let myself experience it.

Like a guest in a foreign country, I watched the cues, hoping to get it right. I put the spoon in my mouth, tasting a subtle, creamy bitterness. Without making a mustard face, I said, "Not bad."

She laughed at me. "You didn't even taste it yet. You tasted hot metal."

I felt like a child pretending to be a grown-up, embarrassed that she had called me out. She could see right through my reluctance.

She handed the mug to me. Now came the moment of truth.

I brought the mug to my mouth, this blend of water, powdery-ground beans, and chocolate-raspberry creamer. Indeed, the mug felt perfect in my hands. And this beverage she had made for me felt personal, curated, and designed with me in mind.

Suddenly I felt nervous. I thought, *I really hope I like this. It will be very embarrassing if I don't.*

I tasted it. And the truth is, it wasn't a bad experience. It was fine. Tolerable. I didn't spit it out. I wasn't used to liking it, but I could see why some people did. Prepared the right way, I conceded, this could be something a person would drink.

She stared at me, waiting for my response. She raised her eyebrows. "Not so bad, right?"

I took another sip.

And that's how I found myself drinking my first cup of coffee.

Let me tell you what it feels like to be groomed by an abuser. It's quite a bit like learning to drink a cup of coffee.

Grooming is a tool that abusers use to gain the trust of their targeted individual, and it's ultimately how they manipulate the victim's trust to gain the advantage. Grooming is not a simple, cookie-cutter technique—it's certainly more complicated than brewing a cup of coffee. And, of course, this metaphor has another obvious limitation: You and I both know that actual baristas have no nefarious intentions as they pour your coffee. But because some of the parallels can help us understand how the process of grooming works, let's walk through how someone gets another person to like coffee.

If you've never enjoyed a cup of coffee, you might think, *Why would someone drink that brown water that doesn't even smell good? I've never enjoyed the flavor at all, and it makes no sense to me. Gross.*

Or, you might wonder, *Why would someone allow themselves to taste something that other people become addicted to?*

Why can't you just drink something else that you know you enjoy? Can't you see what's happening, that they're trying to trick you into liking something you don't?

Let's consider the approach. Skilled baristas know what they're doing. They are coffee mixologists and connoisseurs who have been trained to know which brews partner well with which flavor choices. They have an end goal in mind: to introduce you to something you'll enjoy. It may be something you didn't previously tolerate, and with some focused adjustments, they might even create something you feel you need on a regular basis. You might even learn how to order it for yourself.

Now consider how an abuser works in grooming someone. The abuser wants you to enjoy something you've never liked before, maybe something you've never even tried but that you've perhaps felt curious about. They will ask some questions to measure your interest, and they'll convince you that there's nothing to lose. They will create a personal experience, curated and designed for you. They might even invite you to make a few choices so it feels like you were part of the decision.

A good barista will watch you closely as you take a sip to gauge your reaction so they can make adjustments and know how to help you feel comfortable to try it a second time, then a third. A barista will empower you to believe that if you can try this coffee drink, you can try anything else on the menu.

An abuser, too, will assess your response, and they'll tweak the experience for next time. An abuser will show you that discomfort doesn't have to be a bad thing, that the world won't stop spinning if you let down your guard.

A barista has your enjoyment in mind. An abuser has their own ends in mind.

Both can simply introduce you to something new with the intent to draw you back for more, and that is a powerful skill—one that can be dangerous in the wrong hands. An abuser is not offering, exposing, observing, adjusting for the sake of another person. They're doing it to gain control.

It doesn't happen all in one sitting, believe me. You don't walk into a coffee shop with no interest and walk out with a caffeine addiction. That's part of the brilliance. You don't necessarily even know you're building a tolerance to this thing you once steered clear of. It's a slow process, a few degrees at a time, a slow exposure that desensitizes you to the bitterness until you can't taste it at all.

When an abuser knows what risks you're willing to take, they'll find another reason to pour you another cup. And an abuser can be very, very patient while they learn what you can tolerate. After all, this isn't just a cup of black coffee you could get at any random coffee shop. It's a specialized cup, poured for you. And if you don't like it the first time, they'll find a way you like it.

They'll make you forget you ever disliked it, that you were ever on the outside looking in. They'll make you feel like it was your idea, like they gave you what your tastes wanted all along. They'll make you begin to wonder how well you knew yourself at all.

That's what it feels like. It was never just a cup of coffee.

Jana

If you can get someone to turn their head a little bit at a time, shifting their gaze incrementally, they might not notice that they have gone from looking left to looking right. If you force them to turn too fast, they'll feel it. But if you go slow, one tiny adjustment at a time, then you can get them where you want them. They might not even know they looked away until they're staring at what you had in mind all along.

They might not notice they have changed perspective.

They might not notice they have changed their mind.

They might not notice they have changed.

While manipulation is the art of shifting someone's perspectives and behaviors, it's important to note here that not all manipulation is bad. In fact, some manipulation is very, very good, helpful, and even healing.

According to *Merriam-Webster*, there are several definitions:

manipulate (verb)
1. to treat or operate with or as if with the hands or by mechanical means especially in a skillful manner [as one would manipulate a pencil or machine]
2. to manage or utilize skillfully [as one would manipulate data or statistics to best understand the research][1]

With these definitions, a small child learns fine motor skills as they learn to *manipulate* blocks. A surgeon *manipulates* the mechanical arms of a robot for a state-of-the-art surgery. In a class of young scientists, the students *manipulate* mirrors to experiment with light and color. In medicine, a chiropractor is known to *manipulate* the vertebrae of a person's spine, thereby bringing great relief.

Manipulation can be a very good thing, even a skill.

Consider a typical Sunday morning. Few of us walk into church in a peaceful, readily worshipful state. We're already thinking about the list of things we have to do in the afternoon. Maybe we had an argument on the drive. Maybe we worked late the night before or didn't sleep well. Maybe we have young kids we've been rushing into the car and coaxing into Sunday school.

By the time we get to our seats, we may or may not be on time, we may have just finished whisper-arguing, and we're almost certainly distracted. How does the worship team lead this congregation of distracted individuals into the throne room of God?

Well, it calls for a certain kind of redirection, a skillful management of people and their emotions. Are worship leaders manipulative? We would never say that because it's not what we mean here.

Still, an effective worship experience requires skillful, subtle manipulation over the course of just four or five songs. The worship team begins with an upbeat song that matches the frenetic energy in the room, giving people time to set down their coats and their coffees. With a tone of celebration, the worship pastor brings scattered minds and elevated blood pressure to a manageable pace.

Next, the worship experience slows down a little, but not

too much. We feel the room exhale a little as we remember why we came. The team leads us in a song of how good God is, how kind and faithful, perhaps a prayer to open the eyes of our hearts. And finally, they lead us in a song that will emphasize the theme of the sermon series and prepare us for the pastor's message. Now that they've created an intimate atmosphere in the room, they hand the microphone to the preaching pastor.

The worship pastor manipulates us from a point of stress to a posture of worship. And every Sunday, we thank them for it. They have skillfully shifted our focus from distracted to engaged, from inward to upward, from serving ourselves to worshiping God.

In fact, we all do it to some degree, as a basic part of managing people. There are times when a direct conversation isn't the most direct route to change, so coaches, teachers, and parents practice manipulation all the time. It's how we get children to eat their vegetables, brush their teeth, learn to apologize, and become autonomous adults who contribute to society. It's how life coaches help their clients meet their goals, with a subtle shift toward changing their habits. It's how fitness coaches make great strides with their athletes, by inching their personal records a little at a time. This redirection can let us move people toward what's helpful for them.

So hear this: Not all manipulation is harmful. Exposure to new things isn't always evil or unhealthy. Working out at the gym doesn't feel good at first, but you push through the discomfort to get the endorphins and the results. Becoming comfortable with discomfort is part of working toward a healthy goal. Anyone who has ever tried to make a positive change will encounter resistance.

But *Merriam-Webster* offers a third definition:

3. to change by artful or unfair means so as to serve one's purpose[2]

That's a different level. An abuser manipulates you to become comfortable with discomfort—not for your good, but for their control. An abuser will teach you not to trust yourself. They will teach you to override that very important internal compass—your gut instinct. They'll tell you it's normal to feel scared. They'll remind you that new things don't taste good at first. They'll remind you that when you're on a path to something new, you will bump up against fears that keep you from your true potential. The abuser will convince you that they are more trustworthy than your instincts. And once you believe that your instincts cannot be trusted, it's open season on your psyche.

In the wrong hands, manipulation is a dangerous skill. Masterful manipulation used to be called *brainwashing*. That term has become woefully misunderstood, so we don't use it anymore, but some of the meanings of the word still apply. Its Chinese characters, for example, translate to mean "thought struggle" or "thought remolding."[3] This is what we might describe as *indoctrination*: teaching someone to accept a set of beliefs without question, which requires excessive devotion, persuasion, conversion, and even resocialization. In clinical settings, we call this *coercive control*.

If you can change a person's behavior or values, then you can get them to follow you anywhere, do anything you lead them to do. If they trust you and not themselves, a person will even betray themselves repeatedly to try something that seems strange.

How can we know if manipulation is the normal, innocuous kind or the kind that moves into coercive control? Entrepreneur and author Seth Godin offers this question to test the purity of manipulation: "If the people you're interacting with discover what you already know, will they be glad that they did what you asked them to?"[4]

What Tricia did not know at this point in her friendship with Annie was that Annie had a predatory history, one that involved manipulating, controlling, and using women to harmful ends. If Tricia had known what Annie had in mind, what she had done to other women, would Tricia have been glad to do what Annie asked her to?

Through love bombing, constant heavy communication, and even subtle manipulations like pushing Tricia to drink something she disliked, Annie taught Tricia to ignore her own instincts and boundaries. She enmeshed herself into Tricia's life and disoriented Tricia's reality in imperceptible, progressive ways. These words, behaviors, and actions laid the groundwork to make Tricia question her own understanding of herself. Annie's manipulation was the work of a virtuoso.

With the benefit of hindsight, we can see how even Annie's early actions demonstrated an intent to mold Tricia into a new version of Annie's own image. If only we could have hindsight before abuse escalates, the beginning signs of coercive control would prevent a lot of hurt, a lot of damage, and a lot of trauma. But hindsight is called hindsight for a reason. Our realities only become clear to us in the devastating aftermath.

That's why it is so vital to understanding the patterns of abusers and how manipulation works. It may not prevent us from getting caught in the web, but if we can recognize when someone is distorting reality, we can get free.

FOUR

Secrets

Tricia

When I wouldn't spend the night at her house, even after several invitations, Annie shifted her course. She invited herself to mine.

In that season of my life, I spent my boys' naptimes and my own late nights editing papers for grad students. I was earning extra cash for our young family, but that wasn't the real reason I loved my side gig. As I polished the students' words, I got to read their big thoughts, which I soaked up to a point of absolute sleep deprivation. Late nights of solitude and wordsmithing felt like a shot of energy that fueled me until the next time I could be alone with the words again.

Annie also often did her most creative work at night, so she suggested we pull a late-nighter at the same place. She pointed out that her husband would be home with her children, my husband would be on a business trip, and wouldn't I enjoy the company, the conversation, and perhaps the coffee?

Perhaps I would, actually. And I could provide the coffee. After enough of Annie's cups of coffee, I had decided to purchase a coffee maker of my own.

That night, I put my little children to bed, and I began my late-night work with words. Annie arrived even later into the evening. She made the pot of coffee, I settled into my chair, she settled onto the couch across the room, and we both got to work.

Then, like Marty McFly flipping the switches and turning the dials on Doc's amplifier, she began moving the night through a series of small, discomforting, nearly imperceptible shifts. My brain began to buzz with heightened intuition.

When Annie used the bathroom, she didn't close the door. She talked to me while she used my toilet, toilet paper, sink, soap, and hand towels. We didn't have that level of intimacy with each other, and she was pushing the boundaries. I could feel it.

Annie showed me a text from another friend, a photo of the cocktail of antibiotics that friend was taking for her strep throat and ear infection. I couldn't think of anyone in my life who would be interested in a photo of my doses of medicine, but Annie had women checking in with her like this all the time, with every level of information. Every detail, at any moment of the day or night. She was physically present with me, but she always had her phone in her hand.

Remember, she and I were exchanging fourteen thousand texts a month at this point. I was only one of many women with whom she maintained that level of constant contact.

As the night got later, Annie changed the ambiance, lighting candles and turning on a coffee-shop singer-songwriter playlist. She moved progressively from the couch to the easy chair in the corner of the room to directly beside me in my oversized chair. When our hips and laptops lined up side by side, she put a blanket over her legs and mine.

My intuition buzzed loud, louder, loudest until finally my blood ran cold. All the alarms sounded within me. Abort mission, get out now.

In the next breath, I shut down everything. The music, the coffee, the candles, the forced intimacy. I needed her out of my house, and I asked her to leave immediately. I couldn't explain what had just happened or why it felt weird, but I needed her to leave.

I watched her walk to her car, and I locked the door behind her.

As I lay alone in bed that night, thinking about how far away my husband was on his business trip, I tried to dissect the evening, to figure out what had gone wrong.

I couldn't name it. I couldn't put my finger on it. But the alarms sounded both unique and familiar. I had felt The Feeling at least once before. Where had I heard these sirens?

In a flash, I knew it exactly. I had felt this exact sense of alarm when I was in college, dating a man I needed to break up with. It had hit me like a lightning bolt then, a beam of clarity as I realized that this person was toxic, dangerous, that I needed to flee to the nearest emergency exit.

But that alarm didn't make sense, not for this situation. Annie wasn't a man. And I wasn't dating her.

So I shut down my instincts. I told them to be quiet. Clearly they were wrong this time.

As I began to drift off to sleep, I had one final, nearly audible thought: *She is playing with fire. And you're going to get burned.*

The next morning, after a trip to the library and the park, I put my little boys down for a nap. I was drying dishes in my sunny, yellow kitchen, to this day the happiest kitchen I have ever lived in. I had been to Costco that week, and I had bought a dozen of their giant muffins. I would cut them in half, wrap each in plastic, and freeze them for upcoming breakfasts and bedtime snacks.

I'm telling you this because I was doing the Tuesday morning duties of my life, trying to go about my day. I still couldn't really name what had happened the night before, only that I had felt The Feeling. I wondered if I had over-reacted, wondered if I should be embarrassed. Was that the name of the stone in my stomach?

Annie texted me to say she needed to stop by.

I texted back, "Sure," and I unlocked the front door. She let herself in moments later, walking around the toys on the living-room floor.

I greeted her, trying to keep it light and cool, as if the tension from the night before was something I navigated all the time. As if I were comfortable with her being here, while the discomfort gnawed in the middle of my stomach.

"Hey there," she said, her standard greeting.

"Hey there," I said, drying another mug.

She had two cups from Starbucks in her hands, size venti. She set them on the counter, eyeing the dishes, the muffins, the tea towels. "Quite a domestic situation you've got going on here," she said. "You're a real live Betty Crocker."

I put the mug in the cupboard. "Muffin?" I offered, pointing to the dozen.

"I'd hate for you to open the package just for me," she said.

"My family won't mind," I said. I took a knife from the dishwasher, and I slit a line in the plastic wrap stretched across the dozen muffins. I cut one in half, placed the halves on dessert plates, and put the plates in the microwave for twenty-two seconds.

"It's like you're a pro," she said. There was a condescending tone to her voice, barely audible beneath the compliment.

"Well, you know. We Ohio girls get the job done," I said.

The microwave beeped. I took out the plates, opened the drawer to find two forks, and placed a plate before each of us. She tapped her fork to mine. "Cheers."

We each took a bite.

She said, "Hey, I'm sorry things got weird last night."

I said, "It's fine. I mean, totally okay. It's . . . whatever."

I didn't know how to receive someone's apology back

then, not without absolving, smoothing it over, trying to make it all better.

"No, it made you uncomfortable," she said. "I made you uncomfortable, and I would never do that on purpose. It happens sometimes, and I never mean to do that. I just forget sometimes that not everybody does friendship the way I do."

I took a bite of my muffin, waiting for her to tell me more.

"I mean, I tend to be all in," she said. "I think that's the only real way to do life together. I think it's the way of intentional community, the way of the church."

"Of course, for sure," I said, sipping my Starbucks.

"But not everyone is comfortable with that kind of authenticity," she said. I didn't hear the manipulation in the words then. I only felt inferior.

I reached into the dishwasher for another mug, then realized it was the one she had drunk from the night before. She seemed to notice I was scrubbing it with my kitchen towel like I was trying to remove a stain.

"Listen," she said, "I know it was maybe kind of a lot. I mean, I know I'm kind of a lot."

I polished the coffee mug. "Sure. Me too, right? We all are."

She set down her fork. "I guess I just want to know if I can be myself around you."

"Yes, of course. Of course you can."

She said, "I don't like fake friendships. I don't want to have to figure out what is okay and what is not okay with you. I need to do real life, to be real together. It's not just something I want. It's something I need, if we're going to be friends."

"Yes, of course." I kept saying those same words.

"So I can trust you?"

"Trust me? Yes, of course. Yes, of course you can trust me."

She picked up her fork and took a bite of my muffin. Sharing forks and food. Life together. The church. She was always making her point and pushing her boundary, both at the same time.

"I actually do have a question for you," Annie said. "I have been reading this week about the theology of intercession, about the beauty and worship of praying for one another. Paul wrote this in his letter to Timothy, that prayers and intercessions should be made for all people, especially those in authority, that we may live peaceful and quiet lives in all godliness and holiness."

She did that a lot, quoted Scripture no one could disagree with.

She said, "I've been thinking about how essential it is for leaders—women like you and me—to have someone who will pray for them every day. We could do that for each other. Know each other's stuff, ask the hard questions, commit to pray for each other. Intercessors."

"That sounds like a really beautiful thing," I said.

"It could be . . . if it's real. Between two people who trust each other."

"Right. Yes, of course."

"There is a target on my back, as a leader," she said, "and there will be a target on yours, too, as you grow into your roles as a leader. It would mean everything if I could ask you to pray for me. If I could *trust you* . . . to pray for me."

"Yes, yes, of course." I said those words again, affirming all the things.

But really, who says no to an invitation like that? How could I say no? *No, I don't feel comfortable with this. I can't pray for you. No, there's something weird going on here that I can't name. I'd rather not pray for you.*

That is not a thing that people say. And she knew that.

Abusers in religious contexts, I'd learn later, all seem to innately understand how to use spiritual language. It becomes another tool, another point of leverage.

"So intercessors then?" she asked. "You'll be mine and I'll be yours?"

She raised her Starbucks cup to mine. Cheers, like we were closing a deal.

I raised my paper cup to hers. Cheers, to intercession.

We each took a sip. Closing the agreement.

"So tell me how I can pray for you," I said.

She took a bite of muffin. There were two or three beats of silence.

Then she said, "Well, it does kind of have to do with last night. That kind of thing has happened to me before, where I just get really misunderstood. You're not the first person to respond to me that way. And it's pretty terrible to offer myself in friendship to someone and have them put up a wall like that."

She looked at me pointedly, letting the guilt settle on me—how terrible I had made her feel with all my intuitions and boundary setting, how awful I'd been to ship her out and send her home so abruptly.

She pressed further. "So could you pray about that? Pray that you'll be able to accept me, without judging me, for all that I am?"

That is powerful language to deceive just about anyone into a trap of complicity, I imagine. But to someone chronically dependent on being seen as good and helpful, those words are a magic spell.

Reject you? Judge you? No, that can't be who I am.

Love you? Help you? Yes, I want to do that.

Her words cut to the core of who I wanted to be while simultaneously identifying the shadows I avoided at all costs.

"I can do that," I said.

"You can . . . do what?" she asked, waiting for a verbal commitment.

"I mean, both. I can do both—I can pray for you, and I can accept you."

"Not many people do," she said, seeming to fold in on herself, like an origami of shame. "Especially in the church."

Of course I could help her, and I would.

Of course I could love her in the name of Jesus.

Of course I wouldn't judge her.

Of course I wouldn't reject her like everyone else had.

There had to be a way to set boundaries and still be her friend.

There had to be a way to do this safely. If anyone could thread this needle, I believed I could.

Then she said, "It will make all the difference in this

friendship, if I can know I don't have to hide anything from you. I can just be me, all in, all the time."

I nodded.

"As a measure of accountability," she said, "you can ask me anything, at any time. No secrets between you and me. I mean, we'll keep them from other people, as needed, but we'll be totally open with each other. Seriously. There's nothing you cannot question."

She reached across my kitchen counter and took my hand. She said, "This is how I do friendship. No boundaries. Please don't make me have to figure out where you stand. I need to be able to let down my guard, Tricia. You have to let me be me. This is who I am, and this is what friendship with me looks like. All in, all the time."

I nodded. Of course. Of course. Of course.

She smiled, grabbed her coffee, and left her dishes on my counter.

"And one more thing," she said, pointing to me as she walked toward my front door. "Please don't tell anyone about last night. If you tell anyone, I'm toast."

I've never forgotten how she said that. *Toast.*

Of course, I wouldn't tell anyone. What was there to say, even? What had even happened?

Plus, I was her intercessor now. I had just promised to pray for her, accept everything about her, and—most of all—keep her secrets.

She blew a kiss to me, and she walked out the door.

A few minutes later, she sent a series of text messages to continue the morning's dialogue.

"I found this quote that made me think of you and us: 'Love anything, and your heart will certainly be wrung and possibly broken. If you want to make sure of keeping it intact, you must give your heart to no one, not even to an animal.' C. S. Lewis said that. He's one of your favorites. He's saying that this is the only way to really live. To give your heart away."[1]

And then one more:

"'Behold, I am doing a new thing,' God said to Isaiah. He's saying it to us, too. I'd hate for us to miss what he's doing in his church, in you, and in me."

So I became Annie's intercessor, and she became mine. It's a lot of Christianese as I look back on it now, but because I was her "intercessor," the person who prayed for her, she invited me to be her "accountability partner": the person granted access behind the curtain of her life, expected to ask direct questions and to give feedback. And through it all to keep praying for her . . . and keep her secrets.

Confession and accountability in the family of God can be a good thing, a practice of honesty and compassion, a pathway to restoration and healing. The idea comes out of Hebrews 3:13: "You must warn each other every day, while it is still 'today,' so that none of you will be deceived by sin and hardened against God."

But this was not that kind of accountability. I could ask questions, but she always had a way to redirect the answers. She wasn't interested in the nuances of conviction and change. Instead, she twisted those conversations to weigh me down with more secrets, to convince me that my discomfort was just misunderstanding. As I asked questions about things that seemed questionable, she seemed to have answers for all of them.

I asked her about all the physical affection I saw between her and other women, since it was more than I had usually seen at this level of friendship. She said this was the church. She reminded me of when Paul encouraged the people of the church to greet each other with a holy kiss. She meant it literally.

I asked her about the sleeping arrangements I had observed, the grown-up sleepovers and the open-bed policy. Annie said she craved time alone with her girls. She said she loved sleeping next to someone she loved every night of her life, whether it was her husband or someone else. If her husband was away on a business trip or gone for a weekend in the mountains, she'd invite one of her girls to sleep in her bed with her.

I asked her if her husband ever minded her closeness with other women, if it ever seemed to get in the way of their own intimacy. She said it seemed to help their intimacy, to even enhance their fidelity to each other. She said that women need girlfriends because a husband and wife could never meet each other's every need. She said he loved all her friends, and her friends all loved one another. She said every person she loved understood that they would never be the only one she loved.

She always pointed me back to love. She said that a lot

of my questions were related to laws of the Old Testament, not the grace of the New Testament. She said I shouldn't worry about the things Jesus didn't worry about. She said if I wanted to be more like Jesus, then I should be open to love and more love. She told me verses like "The only thing that matters is faith expressing itself through love."[2] She said that as I matured in my faith I would also mature in my understanding of love, and that would bring some experiences that I would become more comfortable with.

I felt like a child. She teased me that I was a stereotype of conservative evangelicalism, that my questions were so basic. She said I was naive. I felt so much less smart around her, which I figured out later made me vulnerable to suggestions and new definitions. I began to silence my own questions and reservations as she made me question the people who had been my teachers. And in planting doubts and silencing my questions, she isolated me from the people I had trusted.

It's good to wonder, she said. It's good to not know.

It's good to keep tasting new things until you discover you want them again.

As her intercessor and her accountability partner, I learned that she was attracted to women. I learned that everyone who had learned this had cast her away from the church. I learned that the church had let her down, and I wanted to show her that the church could be different. I could hold the information, hold the boundary. She was married to a man but attracted to women, but I wasn't dealing with the same thing. Sexuality wasn't contagious, no more than knowing someone else who was addicted to alcohol would make me an alcoholic.

So I kept her secrets, and I let her silence me.

Jana

Exiled Russian poet Joseph Brodsky said, "You think evil is going to come into your houses wearing big black boots. It doesn't come like that. Look at the language. It begins in the language."[3]

A skilled abuser will use emotional intimacy as protection, aligning the victim with their goals. Using the language of secrets, they make this intimacy sound like transparency, when really it's a drape of darkness.

Swiss psychiatrist Carl Jung writes, "Anything concealed is a secret. The possession of secrets acts like a psychic poison that alienates their possessor from the community."[4]

Wade Mullen provides a helpful dissection of the layers of secret keeping, explaining how they function.[5] The depth and breadth of secrets make them incredibly complex, always more than they seem.

The simplest level of secrecy is a *free secret*, which is a secret that does not "threaten the image of the person holding the secret."[6] Essentially, this information doesn't jeopardize the image of the person holding the juicy information. They heard such-and-such about so-and-so, and they can hold it or pass it along because they have nothing to lose. It's not personally their story, so they feel free to talk about it— often for the ugly thrill of gossip. Of course, we know that gossip risks their integrity, so it does cost them *something*, but they rarely seem to consider that against the reward of the inside scoop. It costs them little to pass this information along because they have no skin in the game.

The next level is an *entrusted secret*, which is still on the safer side of the spectrum of secrets. Entrusted secrets are kept because the nature of the relationship involved requires confidentiality. This might include information between a doctor and patient or between a therapist and client. Even still, the person entrusted with the secret may have a mandated duty to report the secret, especially if the secret involves the abuse or mistreatment of a child, harm to the person themself, or harm to someone else. So there are situations when even the person entrusted with the information may have an obligation to let someone else know.

Inside secrets live on the line between the darkness and the light. These secrets are pieces of information held within a small group of people. An inside secret can be innocuous, such as a few friends planning a surprise birthday party. But sometimes inside secrets foster a sense of exclusivity, of being elite because you're in the know. An abuser will utilize this charade of intimacy as part of the grooming process. They might say to you, "Keep this secret for me, as part of the intimacy of our friendship."

Most complex of all are *dark secrets*. These are the facts that "a person or an organization knows and conceals because if they were revealed, they could damage the image of that person or organization."[7] Dark secrets are private and confidential, usually because the information is embarrassing, incriminating, or shameful.

When Annie shared her "prayer request" with Tricia, she was sharing a secret that had three layers.

First, it was a dark secret. She was a woman with spiritual authority, and she was married to a man. In her specific religious context, the secrets of her attraction to and approaches with women would have threatened her reputation, her marriage, and her livelihood.

Second, it was an inside secret, designed to create a sense of intimacy. She asked Tricia to keep the information as a demonstration of loyalty.

Third, when Annie asked Tricia to be her intercessor, she looped her into an entrusted relationship of secret keeping. If Tricia had been Annie's doctor or therapist, an agreed-upon role with boundaries in place, that would have been one thing. But Annie placed Tricia in a situation where Tricia could not ask for help without breaking a trusted confidence. Annie put Tricia's devotion on the line.

And finally, Annie was in a position of power as a person with spiritual authority. A spiritual leader is a shepherd of sheep, and Scripture is clear that sheep are to be fed, protected, and healed. Diane Langberg, a psychologist specializing in treating trauma survivors, writes, "It is always the responsibility of the shepherd or the one with the power to maintain the integrity of the relationship—the boss, the counselor, the pastor."[8]

Both Annie and Tricia had a strong motivation to hide Annie's wrongs, of which Tricia had only an inkling at this point: that Annie, despite being married, despite having spiritual authority, not only acted on her attraction to people she had authority over but did so in coercive, harmful ways. And many people would be damaged if Tricia shared the secret.

Certainly, Annie's behavior would be exposed, and she would have to deal with the fallout. While Jesus teaches us that we have no right to throw stones, sexual sin—particularly when it involves a power differential—cannot be taken lightly. We cannot ignore it, and we must never hide it.

Certainly, Annie's husband would feel the pain, with his wife's secret life exposed.

Certainly, Annie's children would feel the pain, with their family undergoing scrutiny.

And possibly, the most far-reaching damage might be to the faith of those who had followed someone they thought they could trust.

When Annie asked Tricia to keep her secrets, she isolated her from her husband, family, and close friends, shifting the responsibility of any fallout to her and trapping her in silence. We must never forget that not all abuse is physical. In many cases, deeply harmful abuse may be verbal, spiritual, or emotional. Because the effects of that kind of abuse are seemingly less severe, however, the victim can doubt her reactions in what is called *gaslighting*. Because she is not being physically attacked, she may not be able to explain the abuse to herself or to others.

From a clinical and objective standpoint, as a therapist who has seen the patterns of a lot of abusers, I can say this: Annie's secret was a masterful power play.

The Still before the Storm

Tricia

So why, then, did I keep her secrets?

Perhaps it's time to introduce you to another layer of myself.

My name is Tricia, and I am a recovering codependent. I could cut and paste some wordy scientific definitions of codependency here, but my best definition is simply what it looks like and means for me.

I know I am being codependent

when I am repeating an unhealthy pattern

so I can stay in relationship with someone.

As "a helper," I probably am a delight to have in your life. But the bummer for me is that I'm probably addicted to helping you, rescuing you, and being the hero of your life. And if I'm giving up part of myself to make your life easier, or to keep you from having to deal with some junk you should probably deal with, then I'm doing something unhealthy to myself so I can stay in relationship with you.

When I'm being codependent, I struggle to have a voice of my own. I'm focusing only on what you say, not on my own thoughts or needs. Your feelings seem louder, so they feel more important.

Sorry for the pronouns. It's not really about *you*. It's about *me*.

Codependency can look like selfless thoughtfulness. But it masks the lie that another person's preferences and choices are more important than my own needs, my own voice, my own instincts. In that noise, sometimes we codependents fuel many other addictions of the world, giving people what they want and enabling their sources. We become deceived by an immediate solution to avoid feeling unsafe.

In truth, compulsive helpfulness can become another addiction. If you were to compare each addiction to codependency, weighing them against each other, you'd find that codependency is an equal problem—maybe even the bigger problem, in some cases.

We enable the wrong things for the right reasons.

We just want you to love us. Really, you're our addiction.

That is a painful realization for us all. Especially us codependents.

Add to my codependency the fact that I am also an empath, which means that I feel other people's feelings, whether I want to or not. So that unsafe feeling could be as invisible as picking up on an awkward exchange or a depressed mood in another person in the room. I saw a meme that said, "My ability to 'read the room' is the entire reason I don't like to leave the house." Yes. That.

Put me in a room with any other person, and every social exchange becomes a labyrinth of vigilance as I monitor each person's reaction to every other person's nonverbal cue. And if it's a long exposure to a lot of people, then my brain will spend hours feeling all the feelings in the room. I know it doesn't make sense, and I tell myself it doesn't make sense. This only makes me battle emotions and logic until emotions take over, because ultimately I can't deny that I can sense that the couple over there is processing some kind of tension about something, and I should do something to help them so I can stop feeling their tension. I wish I could turn it off, or even turn it down, but it's how things go for a lot of us codependents. We are forever on alert, lest we miss an important cue and fail at a codependent task.

You might say that sounds like a gauntlet. I call it Thanksgiving. Or Sunday morning.

Connection is the root of codependency, and codependent behavior is an addiction based in fear—fear of losing that connection. That's why many forms of abuse—mental, physical, emotional, sexual, and spiritual—rely on codependency, preying on a person's vulnerability and need for connection to enmesh them in an unhealthy dynamic.

When a victim has been abused, the connection to the abuser replaces their sense of self. Without a lifegiving sense of self, the connection to the abuser feels impossible to exist without.

That's why I kept Annie's secrets. That's why I didn't get out of the friendship even once the alarm bells were blaring constantly. It's the same reason an alcoholic returns to the bottle. The same reason an addict can't walk away. Because the drug of dependency is powerful.

But then, after a few years, something happened to interrupt this chronically codependent friendship with its secrets to keep and its ever-shifting reality. Annie announced that she and her husband were moving.

I had mixed feelings about their family relocating. I felt all the emotions you might imagine when a close friend is about to move away. But also I felt all the emotions you might imagine if you were finally going through withdrawal from an addiction and starting to get glimpses of the freedom on the other side.

In the weeks before she packed up her home, I had a dream.

I was standing in the middle of a cornfield, and an airplane flew overhead through a clear blue sky. Behind the plane trailed a banner announcing to the world *Annie Is Moving Away*.

I read the sign, and I started running. I chased after that airplane, as if I could catch it if only I could run fast enough. I raced through rows of corn. I started shedding things I didn't need so I could run faster. I cast off the dreamy scarf

I had worn around my neck, and then I shed my cute cardigan. I could run without those. I had to catch that plane.

But as the plane flew farther away, the words getting smaller and the reality feeling more real, I got more desperate. I started casting aside things I actually needed, like my shoes, and then my glasses. Things I needed for my actual life.

In my dream, I realized I was never going to catch the airplane. I stopped running with the eventual jog of one who realizes they're losing the race. Even in my dream, I knew I was losing too much of myself.

I woke up gasping breaths of relief. *Okay. It's okay. She's moving away, and it will be okay. Better than okay. I'll get myself back.*

And that's what began to happen. The fog began to clear, just a little. My disorientation started to right itself. I felt like I could breathe again, just a little.

Robb had sensed a weird dynamic, as husbands do. They tend to know which of the wife's friends are in favor of the marriage, and he suspected she had wanted more than either of us wanted me to give her. Anytime he and I talked about the next-level nature of my friendship with Annie, we agreed—it felt demanding and complicated, but severing the friendship had felt like an extreme response. So we both ignored our instincts. I kept my boundary, and I kept her secrets.

A while after she moved away, I visited her in her new town. I met her new friends in her new place. I visited her new church, met her new people, learned the new places of her new community.

And I saw the same things happening. The movie nights with the women. The sleepovers with the blankets. The greetings with the holy kiss. She was creating the same community with the same toxic patterns, in a new place where nobody knew what questions to ask. Nobody knew what she had done before.

I decided I wouldn't visit her anymore. The "life together" terms of our friendship were complete, the chapter was finished, and the season was over. It was a good time to step back. We could be friends from a distance.

Strengthened by the distance from Annie, Robb and I celebrated our tenth wedding anniversary that summer. I remember that we laughed about how much more time we had together now that I wasn't tethered by fourteen thousand texts a month.

Six weeks later, he died.

FIVE

Trauma

Tricia

He died so fast. He was gone in a morning. His spirit slipped through my fingers.

I have begun to hate that I always say it that way, but it's how it happened. It's not a cliché. I felt him leave this earth as I sat on the floor beside him, holding on to his shirt, as if that could make him stay, as if I could keep him there. I couldn't.

A thousand things arrived the same day when everything was lost. Some words arrived I wasn't expecting, like *widow*. I remember saying that word over and over, just to hear it. It felt like a different language, like a word I needed to practice saying because it's something I had become. It was a word that now explained my life.

A lot of food arrived that day. A lot of casseroles. A lot of lasagnas.

A lot of people arrived that day, on the crisis of all crises.

Some people came because they knew what to do, and some people came because they didn't know how to be anywhere else. They came from near and far. They came because they had to be near me, near us, and they just had to be together.

As my family and I called pastors, neighbors, aunts, uncles, and friends near and far, we called Annie. She had been my friend for years, after all. Friends need to know when someone's world falls apart. And so, because we called her, Annie came. She packed a bag and drove the distance to show up the same day.

On the day Robb died, Annie became a fixture at my house, an unquestioned presence, coming and going as she pleased. She ended up staying for months.

The next few days are a blur, all written in another book of mine, *And Life Comes Back*. I'm glad I wrote it then because I couldn't write that story now. Not very well, anyway. Those are words that existed only then and there because I wrote them then and there. The memories have faded now, and that's part of the grace of being in emotional shock. There are things one forgets.

But there are things one remembers, no matter how much time passes.

I remember sitting at the dinner table, planning the details of my husband's funeral.

I remember looking at my options for urns for his ashes, knowing none of them were right.

I remember how it snowed on the day of his calling hours, hosted at a coffee shop he and I had loved.

I remember not being able to sleep. I remember feeling overwhelmed with panic and grief. I remember doctors prescribing medicine to help me with both.

I remember going home the night of Robb's funeral, feeling like it had been my last date with him.

I remember needing to take a bath. My basic skills were gone, including washing my hair and feeding myself. Between the grief and the medication, everything seemed so difficult, so meaningless. My brain and body seemed slow, dipped in thick molasses.

I remember when Annie helped me take a bath. I remember that she took off her clothes, and she got into the tub behind me. She washed my hair, pouring water over my head to rinse out the bubbles. I remember seeing and knowing, from my far, catatonic distance, when she did something horrifically wrong to my body. My self. My soul.

In the remembering, Jana has tasked me with clarifying the difference between a caregiver and a predator. In case you'd like to do the same, minimal research is required.

It's not difficult to offer human decency to a catatonic person who needs help getting clean. A caregiver would offer a robe, ensure the person's privacy, explain what they are doing as they do it, and use a washcloth. A caregiver wouldn't take off her own clothes and join the patient in the water. Without a washcloth or permission. A caregiver would not take liberties with the body of the person who gives no consent.

I will not write all that I remember. Because it's too much for all of us. But in place of all that is true, I read this quote in a *New York Times* book review:

> Whenever there is a horror situation . . . in real life
> or in a work of art, the question arises: Do we require
> the worst details? Why or why not? . . . I tend to agree
> with the critic Clive James, who said that "a scream
> from the other side of a closed door is usually enough
> to convince me."[1]

So I will not write all that I remember. But there was a moment, in the bathtub and afterward in my bed, when I knew it was all too much.

Even I, the seemingly boundaryless, knew she had crossed a line.

Even I, the chronically codependent, knew this was too far.

Even I, sedated and barely conscious, knew I had been desecrated.

I knew she was in complete control.

Every protection was gone. Including my husband.

Jana

Trauma is an act of violence that we cannot stop or regulate. It involves death or serious injury, and our emotions include intense fear, helplessness, and horror. Trauma happens to our friends, our families, and our neighbors. It happens to us because it can happen to anyone.

Over dozens of therapy sessions, Tricia and I have stitched together the events of that week when Robb died, suddenly and unexpectedly. The timeline begins with the earliest symptoms of his illness, their visit to the emergency room, her worry through the night, his sudden turn for the worse and inability to slow down his breathing. We have talked about her efforts to rescue him, her call to 911, and the moment of his passing before the paramedics arrived, when he took his last breath and his soul left his body. The following hours include the tender and horrific moments of notifying his family, saying good-bye to his body, and telling her preschool children that their dad had died. All in a morning, two days before Christmas.

The crisis didn't end that night or the following day. She needed to get out of bed the next day—and the next, and the next—to face a life turned upside down. She planned his funeral, authorized his cremation, and proceeded through the broken motions and shattered traditions of Christmas Eve and Christmas Day. In the week to come, she received hundreds of guests at her husband's calling hours, delivered the eulogy at his funeral, and took the first few steps as the calendar turned to the New Year without him.

All the while, in her waking and sleeping, her brain was processing and replaying the moments before, during, and after Robb's death. She had been the only person there to respond. Her body went into fight mode to call 911; to do CPR; and to respond to protect her husband, her children, and herself. No strength in the world compares to a mama bear's instinct to fight, and Tricia put the pedal to the metal that night.

Let's consider what was happening in her body during this time of crisis as she witnessed and processed this degree of trauma.

Our bodies have been created with elaborate systems designed to help us respond to stress. The human brain is deeply connected to the human body, and in crisis, our stress hormones surge from the brain through the body, with control working from the top down. The systems of a body become like a symphony of instruments: each playing its own part, but all working together in response to the stress. Everything affects everything else.

In this complex nervous system, there are two branches: the sympathetic and the parasympathetic. In normal conditions, they work together, managing the body's energy flow like the stop and start of a car. The sympathetic acts as the accelerator, expending energy to help us quickly respond in moments of stress, crisis, or danger. The parasympathetic serves as the brake, helping us recover energy again when the body is in resting mode. Parasympathetic mode allows the body to heal itself. In normal conditions, this is the dance of work and rest, the balance of stress and sleep.

You can explore your own sympathetic and parasympathetic systems right now, as you're reading this page. Take a deep breath, in and out. When you inhale, you activate the sympathetic systems, giving yourself a burst of adrenaline that speeds up your heart rate. In turn, your exhale slows down the heart. If you take a yoga or meditation class, your instructor will bring your attention to the exhale, since deep long breaths out will calm you down.

Imagine this: In the week that Robb died, Tricia's brain was stuck on the inhale.

Her body and her brain could not calm down on their own. Every time she closed her eyes, Robb was dying in her arms again. Every time she tried to sleep, she had to try to rescue him again in her dreams. Her brain replayed the trauma like a record player needle stuck in a scratched record, repeating the worst moments of her life on an endless loop.

She couldn't switch into parasympathetic functioning for several days, and then only with medication to help her settle and sleep. Her medical team prescribed sedatives and sleep aids, and finally she was able to rest for a little while at a time, for a few minutes or a few hours.

While Tricia was under the effect of those sedatives, Annie sexually assaulted her, multiple times.

In the textbook nature of trauma, it is impossible to identify if the assaults began within the first twenty-four hours after Robb's death or within the first week. But the specificity of the timing hardly matters. The damage happened during the worst week of Tricia's life, when her body was in recovery mode from unspeakable trauma, when her parasympathetic system should have been in charge, when she should have been safe.

This kind of trauma upon trauma teaches a person's brain that it cannot exhale. The brain stays heightened, unable to take a breath from this duty of hypervigilance. When the body is attacked at rest, it adapts by learning not to rest. Just as an object in motion will stay in motion, a body stuck in trauma cannot heal.[2]

Traumatized people recover in the context of relationships: within their families, friend groups, support groups, communities, and with professional therapists. The role of these relationships is to come alongside the person, to face the reality of what has happened to them, to protect them from shame or judgment, and to provide both physical and emotional safety. Recovery from trauma involves connecting with people, since the traumatized person needs to be seen, soothed, and protected by another person. When the opposite happens, the pain is compounded on a neurobiological level.

This is why trauma that occurs in relationships can be more difficult to treat than trauma resulting from car accidents or natural disasters: because when your caregiver turns on you, relationships are no longer a place for recovery. You have to find alternative ways to deal with feeling afraid or angry. Managing this level of terror all by yourself gives root to another set of problems: despair, addictions, disconnection, dissociation, and a chronic sense of panic, all of which I saw present in Tricia. Patients with these traumas rarely connect the dots between what has happened to them and how they currently feel and behave; they simply feel like their lives are out of control.

People who respond this way to trauma are not going crazy, and they are not weak. Sometimes painful memories get stuck, through no fault of the victim. The violence of trauma affects our psyches, our relationships, and our bodies, and the spectrum of trauma is deep and wide.

These painful memories can effect real biological changes that produce physical changes and even illness, known as PTSD. Up to 6 percent of people in the United States will experience PTSD at some point in their lives,[3] and probably anyone would develop PTSD if they experienced a severe enough trauma.

Most of the time, PTSD is generally related to a single traumatic event because just one traumatic event can have a tremendous and long-lasting impact on our lives. But there is a next-level variation as well, known as complex PTSD. According to the Center for Treatment of Anxiety and Mood Disorders, "Complex trauma occurs repeatedly and often involves direct harm to the victim. Its effects are cumulative and generally transpire in a specific setting and, frequently, within a particular time frame or within a specific relationship."[4]

Complex trauma can be two traumas happening at once, which happened to Tricia.

Complex trauma can also be one abuse, grooming, and sexual mistreatment happening over and over, which happened to Tricia.

Robb died two days before Christmas. I met Tricia a few weeks into January, after many devastating layers of damage had been done.

On the first day Tricia and I met, I didn't know the whole story yet, but I recognized that her symptoms aligned with complex PTSD. Tricia was in a continual state of high alert, always afraid and anxious. She struggled to make simple decisions, overwhelmed by the simplest choices. She told me she had difficulty sleeping, and I could see her having a hard time concentrating.

When we talked about the week Robb died, Tricia's memories of that week returned as flashbacks with fragments of experiences—isolated images, sounds, and body sensations without context. She felt dizzy or nauseous when she recalled the trauma, and she could not regulate her emotions very well. She said she had lost her trust in herself, her friends, and the world. She felt helpless and hopeless, like she was in danger, always.

She became fatigued in conversation. Her brain was constantly evaluating signs and signals, causing her to need three or four days to recover from a simple coffee date with a friend. Each social interaction was the equivalent of unplugging a smartphone while the battery is still in the red. She couldn't recharge, which makes sense. If you're trying to navigate using a GPS on a phone that's spinning to find a signal it can count on, eventually you won't have enough juice to even make a phone call.

Tricia was overstimulated by the millions of bits of information passing through her brain every second. The brain reacts to every sensory input, from the position of your elbow to the wind in your hair. It's all data that the brain processes as noise. A healthy brain is constantly processing new experiences through memories of past experiences, looking for how they are connected, and if we sense an emotional change in the room that's associated with a memory, we feel that emotion all over again. A person with PTSD has a brain working on hyperdrive, and it no longer has a filter to tame this endless input. The sensory overload is constant. This hypervigilance may be conscious or unconscious, but either way, it's exhausting.

Ideally, a healthy stress-hormone system should respond lightning fast to a threat, and then it should dissipate and quickly find its balance. But the stress hormones of traumatized people take much longer to return to normal. The signals keep firing long after the danger is gone. This endless release of stress hormones emerges as agitation and panic, which soon begins to wreak havoc on the traumatized person's physical health.

I've seen a body enduring nonstop stress compared to a nation during wartime. The resources go to fighting the enemy abroad, leaving the homeland vulnerable to attack.[5] Tricia's body was focusing on her grief and trauma and overwhelm, and it had no remaining sources to allocate toward immunity.

In that first year, Tricia was admitted to the emergency room six times. Sometimes for anxiety from which she could not recover, and twice for dehydration when she could not stop throwing up. Her once-healthy immune system was now compromised, leading to migraines, chronic pain in her body and joints, and the inability to fall asleep on her own. Her body began to break.

But I also saw a spark within her, a small flame that needed to be protected before it blew out completely. I had to triage and start with the most emergent issue: Our first task together had to be to address her grief and stabilize her so she could function.

Even without knowing the whole story, I could help her. Even before she could name the terrible things that had happened to her, I could help her gain mastery over the sensations of her body and the emotions of her mind.

I could teach her coping tools and breathing skills to use when she felt panic rising while driving her sons home from preschool.

I could teach her how to baby-step a trip to the mailbox, or even delegate tasks like shopping at the grocery store, which felt overstimulating with people, music, and dozens of choices for cereal alone.

I could help her stay in the moment, understand that flashbacks are memories revisited, not danger returning. I could help her recognize anxiety as an emotion that will pass like any other. We don't stay mad forever, excited forever, happy forever, or anxious forever.

I could help her expect less from herself and celebrate the small victories.

Every minute of every day, she was worried about her little boys. I could help her manage the scope of their wellness by defining it differently: The healthiest thing for her children was having a healthy mom.

I could not change what had happened. None of it could be undone. But I could help her manage the effects. Trauma takes away this feeling of knowing yourself, of having any sense of control of what happens to you. When a person is repeatedly coerced, bullied, gaslit, manipulated, or abused, life can start to seem impossible, and they might feel helpless, hopeless, and overwhelmed. This is where therapy comes in. Thankfully, the help available today for a person who has been through trauma is far more effective and compassionate than it was even a few years ago.[6]

For Tricia, our first order of business was to deal with the immediate needs, to find ways to cope with feeling overwhelmed by the sensations and emotions of what had happened to her. Sensing, naming, and identifying what is going on inside is the first step to recovery. Tricia and I had a lot of work to do to reestablish her sense of ownership over her body and her mind—her entire self.

And so we got to work.

SIX

Untangling Shame

Tricia

I feel like I can guess what you're thinking, because it's a thought I've had to unlearn as well.

For a long, long time, I told myself, *Tricia, you should have told her no. You should have denied her access to you. You should have set a boundary, and you should have run away. You should never have let this happen to you. Not then, not ever.*

And that is what I should have done. I wish I had known how to do that.

When we are in a right frame of mind and can identify that someone has done something abusive or neglectful to us, then we can immediately recognize that we deserve better. We can take a stand to avoid returning to that abusive situation. We can focus our energies on healthy responses, on corrective behavior, on limits and boundaries. When we are in a healthy frame of mind, we move toward healthy choices.

But I was not in a healthy frame of mind.

First of all, logistically speaking, I was on a lot of drugs to help me get out of bed and a lot of drugs to help me to get back to sleep.

Everything hurt. My shoulders ached when I opened a pill bottle. My arms ached when I lifted a cup of coffee. My head felt like a bowling ball on my shoulders. Everything hurt at least a little, and some parts of me hurt a lot. Not only did I not have the strength for the fight, but I couldn't bear to lose one more thing.

Annie was my friend, and some of her support was keeping me alive, clean, fed, and functioning. She was giving me my medicines,[2] taking me to the doctor, and even driving me to Jana. She did some truly terrible things to me, but other times, she was also very kind and helpful. That's why they call it the *cycle of abuse*: because it isn't all bad. When your friend is also your abuser, it's hard to understand what begins and ends where. That is the nature of crossed boundaries and blurred lines.**

Still, I wish I could tell you that I woke up from the fog of it all, fought for myself, and ended my friendship with her. But I didn't. Even once I realized where I had landed,

---

** I see it now. I do. She was giving me the very medicines to induce my stupor that put her in charge.

what had happened to my body and my life, I didn't leave immediately. I didn't make her stop.

When I asked her to help me understand what this was, she gave me the same lines she had given me before: This was the church. This was unity. This was sharing everything we had. This was life together. She reminded me: This was how she did friendship.

So even once I realized what was happening, I let it happen. I laid down my guard. I gave up the fight.

One specialist explained that my husband dying in my arms was the equivalent trauma to my brain of a car-accident trauma to my body. If what had happened to my soul and my mind had happened to my body instead, he said, I would have spent weeks or months in the intensive care unit. My only responsibilities would be eating, sleeping, and recovering.

That made sense to me because being with Annie was like being in the hospital. Someone was caring for me, and that person had the power to keep me from feeling the carnage of my soul being torn in half. Given the choice between the numbness she offered me and the pain of my life, I chose to let her do what she wanted to do.

I was lonely and heartbroken. She had convinced me that she was a drug to numb the pain. I would have taken any drug at all, and she was the one available to me. All this further twisted my perception in Annie's favor, until I thought, *I chose this.*

Long after she had gone back to her own home, I spent months living in the shame of that lie. For a long time, Annie let me believe the lie, and she perpetuated it.

That kind of toxic shame pulls a person hostage. It overtakes our lives, undermines our willpower, and takes away our ability to stand up for ourselves. That kind of shame can silence a person.

I isolated from my family and friends. I hid my text messages, emails, and interactions like an alcoholic hiding vodka in the tank behind the toilet. The people who loved me suspected I wasn't safe, and I hid all the clues to prove it. A silent breach opened between us where I had placed this barrier of shame.

In my recovery, I have studied the work of Dr. Joy Skarka, whose doctoral research explores how Christian women have experienced sexual shame and how they have experienced freedom.[1] Dr. Skarka surveyed more than one thousand women who were suffering under the weight of sexual shame. *One thousand.*

Consider that number for a moment, please. Imagine them together in one place. The very idea of being one of those women, of standing with them, made me feel less alone.

Dr. Skarka's results revealed this common truth: "Because of sexual shame, women frequently felt far from God, lived a secret life, avoided prayer, and doubted that God loved them."[2]

And I thought it was just me.

After Annie began abusing me, I experienced something new: utter silence from God. Pastor and professor Tim Keller gives this a name of its own: He calls this the torture of divine silence.[3] It felt like the emptiest of voids within me, like calling into a canyon but hearing no echo. The sounds fell dead.

I couldn't summon a response at all. The voice of the One I trusted was absent. Where I had always been able to sense the Holy Spirit, now I heard nothing.

I had always been able to feel that intuition of mine, razor-sharp and often accurate, an inner compass that kept me aligned. I had been able to tell if I was safe, if an environment was safe, or if the air was shifting like in a thunderstorm and I needed to take shelter. I could pause and listen, settle in with the deep knowing, and know what to do next. I had once known the prickly awareness of my instincts, and I'd learned how to wrap that part of my soul in cotton.

The needle of my inner compass lay still like the hands of an abandoned clock. Nothing.

I couldn't feel a single thing.

That's when I knew I had to tell Jana.

"I think I may have had an affair with a woman," I said to Jana. We were outside her office, on a walk in the sunshine for my hour of therapy.

By then, Jana had been my therapist for almost a year, and we had been talking for several hours a week, but I had never told her the full story of what had happened months before.

In all our hours together, all my truth telling, I had never, ever mentioned one word of this secret to her. She knew all the things—except for this one thing I wouldn't tell her. And I was learning this proven truth: When there is one thing I do not want to tell Jana, it is the thing I absolutely must tell her.

We were walking at a fair pace, probably slower than she liked but definitely faster than I liked, taking soft right turns at the stop signs and loops through cul-de-sacs of the neighborhoods around her office. I recall a tricycle in a driveway and a hopscotch path drawn in sidewalk chalk.

When I said that sentence to Jana, the one sentence I had not been able to say, I so startled her with this curveball that she missed a half step in her walk beside me. It took that half second for her to match my stride, to regain pace with my thoughts. A half second.

I have this memory from second grade, when my friend Andy taught me how to shuffle a deck of cards. He was the only seven-year-old I knew who had mastered the bridge shuffle, where you arch the cards back over themselves and they order in place with a most satisfying riffling sound. I've never forgotten that sound, nor how I envied Andy for making his hands do what mine could not.

In the soundtrack of my imagination, that half second plays with that same riffling sound as a deck of cards falling into place. That's how long it took for the pieces of my story to order themselves, for her to see all the things I was saying in that sentence I had never said.

In that half second, it all came together, why some parts of the therapy had worked and others had not. In the giant puzzle of my story, I had been secretly pocketing this dark shadow of a piece, never letting her have all the information, hoping she could heal me without it.

"Okay," she said. "Let's talk about that."

Jana

I met Annie one time, and the interaction and dynamic I observed made me question immediately whether Annie was a safe person. But this was early into my time meeting with Tricia, when Tricia and I were working to build trust as a therapist and patient. I chose not to ask too many questions because we had more emergent issues to address—but I made a note to explore this later.

Later, when Tricia shared with me the whole story of what had happened, I had lots of questions. Still, I couldn't ask them all in one day. You cannot drill a patient with interrogation or they will shut down. A mentor of mine taught me this: "Truth, like love and sleep, resents / Approaches that are too intense."[4]

On the day Tricia told me about the abuse, our work shifted from grief recovery to include therapy for sexual trauma and recovery, but we had to move slowly. If complex trauma is like a ball of knotted, tangled yarn, then we could only unwrap a bit at a time. Pulling and yanking would only make the knots tighter and more difficult to unwind. The work of emotional healing requires a careful, cautious untangling. The patient needs to tolerate feeling what they feel and knowing what they know, and that in itself is a gradual process. Tricia had just unlocked a giant piece of information for both of us.

Sexual trauma grows in the soul like a cancer. Not a surface cancer, like a mole that can be sliced off during an in-office procedure without repercussions. It is more like a deep cancer with tentacles, stretching into the nerves of the brain. The healing is slow and strategic, and it may take months or years to dissect. It is so delicate. If the cancer is attached to other things, then the slightest mishap or movement can damage the person in irrevocable ways.

If you go too fast, sure, you might get rid of the cancer, but you might do so much damage that the patient can no longer speak.

I write this as a specialist in trauma recovery but also as a breast-cancer survivor. People with cancer want it taken away immediately, as soon as they hear the word. But cancer is tricky, sneaky, and deceptive. The specialists have to ask a lot of questions before they can go in to remove it.

In fact, they often won't say *cancer* for a long time. When I went in for a mammogram, the radiologist said only, "I think there's something here." Her flags were up, but she didn't draw any conclusions that day. She sent me for a biopsy that would reveal empirical evidence, then the radiologist sent the sampling to the pathology lab, and then a pathologist analyzed the cells under a microscope. The pathologist was the one who determined that I definitely had cancer.

Even still, the next step wasn't to remove it, only to look closer at it through an MRI. More tests, more details, more blood work, more specifics, more layers. There's a process and a protocol before anything has a name. It sounds repetitive because it is.

My doctors likely knew from the beginning that I had cancer, but they would not verify my diagnosis until they had as much accuracy as possible. There is clarity in the science of protocol.

Thorough emotional healing also requires a process and a protocol. There is a protocol that is true across the board, but it differs with each person, depending on their timing and how well they can cope and process information in their traumatized state.

No one knowingly signs up to be manipulated, or even believes that they can be manipulated. The simple realization that you have been manipulated is often a shock to a person, and it can be painful to acknowledge or realize that you've been betrayed in what looked like a friendship. The normal responses to this kind of trauma include first shock and denial and then grief responses of hurt, guilt, shame, fear, and anger.

The whole time I was working with Tricia, I was assessing her process and her progress. *Where is she today? What can she handle? Where is she in her process? Where is she in healing? What is too tender to talk about, based on what I can see in the moment she enters the office for each session?*

Once she could recognize the complexities of what had happened, then she could begin to identify the unfairness of the ways she had been betrayed and exploited in the most vulnerable season of her life.

So yes, I suspected something strange from the first time I met Annie. But until I had more pieces, and until Tricia's thoughts and heart were prepared to identify and deal with those pieces, we would address only one piece at a time.

One of those pieces was her shame around staying in the

dynamic with Annie even once she realized what was happening. She named it an "affair" when she first told me, but my instincts immediately were that there was more going on. The symptoms of her complex trauma and the information she began to reveal helped us give it its correct name: abuse.

Trauma will trigger people to do things they never would have done if the trauma had never happened. When we are afraid, we seek attachment. We will cling to whatever is close, even if that source of comfort is also the source of harm. If you're not in trauma, it doesn't make sense. But that's because you're not in trauma.

We see this with hostages who have paid bail for their kidnappers. Victims of domestic violence who cover up for their abusers. When my husband served as a police officer, he felt frustrated and powerless when he tried to protect victims of domestic violence and maintain their restraining orders, only to find out that many of the victims secretly allowed their partners to return after my husband left the scene.

How could something so strange happen? When a victim seems to enable or support their abuser, those behaviors are much more complex than the simple choices they appear to be. In fact, these behaviors are not choices at all; they are predictable reactions to the difficult people who caused trauma. When trauma is caused by another person, the cycle of abuse and its effects on the brain can create a bond between victim and perpetrator.

The cycle of abuse is one lens through which we can understand how abusers work. In this cycle, the abuse is not constant but rather moves from an incident of abuse into a period where the abuser attempts to smooth things over, through means such as love bombing, making excuses, apologizing, or denying or downplaying what happened. Once the victim is disoriented and the abuser has sufficiently rewritten reality, the abuser can build back up to another abusive incident.[5]

From a neurobiological perspective, the cycle of abuse elevates both stress hormones and bonding hormones— remember, the abuser is both the source of the pain (stress) and the solution (bonding). Abuse traps the victim's brain in confusion. Even though the perpetrator is toxic and unsafe, they exude power and strength. Even though the perpetrator causes harm, they also soothe the pain they cause. To the victim, the abuser may feel like protection. To the victim, the abuser may feel like the only choice.[6]

Many victims feel an agonizing shame from the actions they took to survive, and then even more shame because of the connection they maintained with the person who abused them. Especially if the abuser was close to the victim, someone they relied on, the victim might feel confused about whether they were a victim or a willing participant. This muddies the margin between feelings and fear, between pain and pleasure.

When people feel shame or guilt, or if something feels overwhelming, it's not uncommon for them to withhold information from their therapist. They are in protective mode, so of course they don't want to talk about it. People will slow down their healing or even subconsciously sabotage their own therapy if they are afraid.

That's why the trust relationship between therapist and client is so vital. A person who has been abused needs to feel safe if they're going to be able to share fully. Safety and trust create the space for untangling shame.

In that space, knowledge becomes a powerful tool, giving a person the language to understand what happened to them and a framework to explain their involvement. When someone understands that these kinds of abusive, toxic, and coercive relationships are common enough to have been studied, and the behaviors are present often enough to have become patterns, they can begin to dissect the many elements and thereby start to separate themselves from the false beliefs underpinning their shame.

So how do people get trapped—and then why do they stay—in an abusive dynamic?

People stay because they still believe in the goals of the person. Decent and honest people presume that others are also decent and honest. When you believe in a cause or a person, this affects your behavior and your actions. Tricia believed Annie's mission and words about the church to still be true. She believed in Annie as a woman of influence, and she responded to Annie's confidence in her. As trauma causes a person to do things they never would have done, loyalty causes a person to stay when they would have otherwise fled.

People stay because most of us, especially in the church, have been brought up to respect authority figures, leaders, and people who give us answers. We are trained to trust people who should know better, and Annie seemed like someone who should know better. She was highly intelligent with advanced degrees. There were other women involved in Annie's life, women whom Tricia knew and trusted. If they were in Annie's life, couldn't Annie be trusted?

People stay because they are exhausted and confused. Tricia was living in a fog from the trauma of Robb dying. In that kind of trauma, all you want to do is make it through each day, so you trudge along, one moment at a time. You're not thinking about the next moment; you're making it through this one.

People stay because they are afraid. Tricia was reeling from an abandonment wound, and she didn't feel like she could survive the loss of one more thing. Annie swept into that vulnerable place.

People stay because they don't know the way back to where they once were. Tricia no longer had very much access to the life she once knew, and this worked very nicely for Annie. As Annie isolated Tricia and removed her from contact with people who had known her and Robb, Tricia in many ways began to forget the person she had been. Trauma erases who we have been, and abusers brush away the eraser marks with their coercive influence.

People stay because they have become dependent. When Tricia's friendship with Annie began, Tricia was a completely independent, autonomous individual. When Robb died and Annie swept in to take over in every way, Tricia became dependent on Annie for her social needs, family needs, self-image, and survival. She became so dependent on Annie that she found the idea of her independence totally confusing and unbearably overwhelming. How could a person in that state of mind draw those kinds of boundaries while she was being led to believe she couldn't function without Annie's help?

People stay because they can't think clearly.

People stay because they don't have the confidence to leave.

People stay because they're afraid of the world, of themselves, of being lonely.

People stay because they feel weak, because they don't know what else to do.

People stay because they think it's their fault.

People need to hear this truth, and we need to tell them:

When abuse occurs, it is the perpetrator's fault.

It is never the fault of the victim.

I wanted to help Tricia understand why she stayed, why she did what she did, how Annie had made her believe what she did. Her free will was not necessarily taken away, but it was distorted and restricted. She was functioning under the duress of what the legal world calls *undue influence*. She was enveloped by a powerful combination of forces that were in many ways totalistic, manipulative, and harmful. Until she could grasp the enormity of that situation, she would continue to doubt herself rather than have compassion for herself.

There is no magic wand, no pixie dust, and no fast-forward button past this process. Healing is always a response to the Holy Spirit, and his work is not usually quick. That is because his work is intentional and deep and lasting.

Healing cannot be rushed, but it will happen when we trust the God of the process.

SEVEN

Ending the Silence

Tricia

I know almost nothing about the sport of rugby, but I fell in love with it because of two words: *with you.*

In case you are as unfamiliar with rugby as I am, please join me for the results of a quick Google tour. The ball is never passed forward down the field, or "the pitch," like in soccer. The ball can only be passed backward or perpendicular, so when the player with the ball runs down the pitch, his teammates fan out behind him, waiting for the pass. All the while, the ruggers shout at the top of their lungs, "With you! With you! With you!"

Their teammate can't see them, so they make sure he hears

them. With two words, they're saying, "I have your back. I'm ready. I'm here. I'm in this *with you*."

In my experience, that is where healing begins too. In the slow and steady kindness of "with you."

To be sexually assaulted or abused is to be treated with an enormous measure of unkindness. The one who is recovering needs an extraordinary amount of patience, and Jana was present in the slow, steady way of kindness. She was *with me*, and she would be with me as long as it took.

She was consistent in her response: "This was wrong. It's wrong morally, but it's also wrong personally. What was done to you was wrong on a personal level. You were violated. She violated *you*."

A person who has been abused needs to hear this. I listened to her every time. I believed her sometimes.

My relationship with Annie had changed in the months since Robb died. After a long time staying in my home, she had gone back to her new home in her new town. I resolved that I wouldn't be alone with her ever again. But I maintained contact with her, checking in with her and letting her check on me.

I watched from a distance as she targeted other women in the same way she had targeted me. I watched her choose and acquire. She had an addiction, and she was in deep. Her methods kept working.

In a text, Annie called me her "precious girl." Autocorrect changed it to "previous girl." Autocorrect has a Freudian accuracy sometimes.

Why didn't I sever everything once I comprehended what

was going on? Because I still felt responsible for her. The church had failed her. She had told me so herself. I wanted to be the one to do this differently. I thought I was *with her*, the way Jana was *with me*.

So I let my abuser have access to me. I thought I had to. I thought it's what Jesus would do.

I have made a list of the things I didn't know then.

- I didn't know then that *no* is a full sentence.

- I didn't know then that when someone doesn't respect the word *no*, they are not respecting your consent.

- I didn't know then how a manipulator can trap someone in unhealthy patterns and places, simply by making the word *no* seem selfish and upsetting.

- I didn't know then that if someone feels ashamed when I won't do what they've asked me to do, that doesn't mean I have shamed them. When Annie told me that my *no* harmed her, made her feel ashamed of who she was, I believed her. I believed her feelings were my fault.

- I didn't know then the patterns of codependency. I didn't know it was a thing to want something for someone more than they want it for themselves.

- I didn't know then that someone can weaponize shame to run over someone else's *no*.

I had said no to Annie in so many ways. But it never seemed to be loud enough, sure enough, locked tightly enough.

But isn't one *no* enough?

It should be. It should have been. I should not have had to keep saying no. Not when I was reeling from Robb's death, when I was barely conscious, when I couldn't function independently to feed and bathe and comfort myself. My *no* should have been enough.

There was a time when I had known the right thing to do, before rightness had been obscured. On that very first night she was in my home, when all the alarms sounded and I knew she had to leave. I had trusted my instincts and honored my own boundaries. There was a time when I had the ability to be that person. Where had that clarity slipped off to?

With that question, another layer of shame crept in. When grooming and manipulation and abuse and assault lead to staying in the abuse, even once you begin to wake up to what's happening—is that sin? Is that enabling the abuser? Is there complicity, culpability, something to own?

Jana had been telling me this was not my fault, but for some reason, her words weren't enough for me. I dismissed her expertise, finding that I could diminish her informed perspective for any number of reasons. I could explain it all away. She was doing her professional due diligence. She liked me, she was kind to me, and she didn't want to give me more to process on top of so much grief.

My therapist could see that I had been manipulated by a masterful abuser, and still the shame lingered. Maybe shame doesn't respond well to kindness. Perhaps shame demands to be punished.

I needed to reckon with my spiritual questions of guilt,

sin, shame, and maybe even penance. I felt a deep longing to hear from someone in the church. The wounding had come from someone with spiritual authority, so the healing needed to involve someone with spiritual authority.

I wanted a second opinion.

I went to my pastor.

My pastor sat in his chair and steepled his fingers as he listened to my confession. When I finished, he asked me, "Did you enter this relationship with your consent?"

I thought about my constant stream of *no*s, the boundaries pushed and prodded over and over, the desecration in my most vulnerable moment. I thought about what Jana had taught me about the premeditation of an abuser, how Annie knew what she was doing far before I knew what she was doing. I thought about the numbness after the assaults, the disorientation, the bone-deep weariness, and the feeling like I had nowhere else I could go and nothing else I could do.

No, I did not consent to this.

"Did she ask you to keep secrets that would have destroyed her family and her career?"

I thought about the night I made her leave, about "If you tell anyone, I'm toast." I thought of what Jana had taught me about the dark secrets and inside information, about how Annie had trapped me in a web of intercession and secret keeping.

Yes, the information she'd asked me to hold would have been destructive.

"Did you have a choice?"

I thought of how Annie had manipulated my intuition, teaching me that my instincts weren't voices to trust in my decision making. I thought of how she twisted Scripture to her advantage, making me wonder if maybe I had been taught the wrong truth about so many things. I thought of how she told me this intimacy was the way of the church, that the only real choice was to obey—or not to obey—the laws of love. I thought about what Jana had taught me about undue influence, about coercive control, about the effects of sedatives and sleep aids. I thought about how I had learned that accountability becomes complicity only when you have all the information.

No, I did not have a choice.

He asked other questions about consent, about power imbalances, and about timing. He listened, he was quiet, and he thought.

Then he said, "Tricia, an affair is a mutual agreement, not a power play with only one person in charge. She knew what she was doing, long before you knew. That's what a predator does. This was patient and premeditated and calculated. She waited for her moment, and I'm sorry to say, but with the death of your husband, she was handed a perfect storm."

He leaned forward, his elbows on his knees, his eye contact intentional. He said, "It stops today, Tricia. You are safe now."

I remember crying at the relief of those words.

He said, "Today, you will send an email to her, severing all contact. She may not contact you in any way, through any avenue. Copy me on that email, and she will know you are no longer alone in this. If you hear another word from her—ever, in any way—then you and I together will contact her employer and report this abuse."

I followed his instructions that day. That was the last time I talked to Annie.

He showed me the way out, actual steps to take to break the chains she had on my life. I think back on it often, the day he said, "It stops today, Tricia. You are safe now."

The strangest thing happened when I brought my shame into the open.

I didn't die. I actually began to heal.

Jana

Tricia and I had discussed many difficult and direct things, including her sexuality. If this relationship with Annie had been an exploration of Tricia being gay, then we would have addressed what that meant, what it would look like, and what it would mean for the next chapter of her life. I would have been remiss as her therapist not to ask those questions, and we had had those direct conversations. But when it came to the hard questions of her culpability, particularly in light of her spiritual context, she wanted a second opinion. Everyone is always entitled to one.

When Tricia's pastor confirmed that she had been the victim of abuse, the target of a predator, I do believe she believed me for the first time. She began to see the truth: All along, she had been a butterfly caught in the web of a black widow.

When Tricia went to her pastor, he got an essential piece

right that too many get wrong: He did not victim blame. Let's talk about this.

Victim blaming is the practice of questioning what the victim could have done differently to prevent a crime or offense from happening. It implies that the fault of the crime lies with the victim, rather than the perpetrator. Victim blaming is sometimes more subtle than overt, and people may lean toward blaming the victim without even realizing they are doing it.

Questions like *What were you wearing?* or *Why were you alone with them?* are examples of blaming the victim.

Statements like *You should have been more careful* or *That would never have happened if you had left immediately* are examples of blaming the victim.

A person shouldn't have to "be more careful" or "leave immediately" in order to stay safe from the harmful choices of another person.

When abuse occurs, it is the perpetrator's fault.

It is never the fault of the victim.

Being the target of a perpetrator's manipulation and abuse is traumatic in itself, but being blamed for the perpetrator's actions, even subtly or unconsciously, may lead a victim to feel as if they are under attack once again. The risk of victim blaming is the reason a lot of people live in their shame for far too long as it cycles into further depression, anxiety, and post-traumatic stress.

Tricia's pastor did not victim blame. He clarified who

was at fault, and he helped Tricia cut off contact so that her abuser would be dissuaded from reengaging. He partnered with her to guarantee her safety.

When cutting off ties with an abuser in your life, there are actual steps to take to keep yourself safe.

- First, if you're living in the same physical location, it's important to prepare to exit. Tricia was not living with Annie, so she didn't need to take some of these steps. But when I worked in a women's shelter, helping women flee abusive relationships, we asked important questions before we helped the women mobilize: Did you collect all the paperwork you would need for you and your children? Did you get money? Do you have clothes for you and your children?

- Next, even if you don't live with the abuser, you still need to have systems in place to protect yourself. Have a support system you can trust, people who will not reveal your location. Do you need to get into a shelter? Get out of state? Go to a friend who can protect your safety and anonymity? Know your safe place, and know your safe people.

- Make a list of your friends. Make a map. How are people connected? Where do they cross over, including social-media connections? People who overlap may not be safe. If they have contact with that person, they are not safe for you. They may reveal things about you. You may need to put boundaries up with other people, those who cross over in the space between you and your abuser. If your social circle is enmeshed in theirs, you may need to sever connections with people who were connected to them. On social media, use the Block button as needed.

A previous victim of Annie's set this perfect example for Tricia. When Tricia reached out for guidance on how to get out of this toxic web, the survivor said, "I want to talk to you, but I can only talk to you if you are not talking to her." That is the kind of protection I am talking about. Know your safe place, and know your safe people.

People may choose to protect you, and they may choose not to protect you. You need to be safe, emotionally and physically. You need to be safe always. Sadly, this means that your world may get very small for a while. Let go of anyone who will not keep you safe.

As Tricia distanced herself from Annie, she stopped hiding. She stopped trying to carry this burden on her own. And in the paradox of surrender, she found freedom. After that day, I saw a lightness in Tricia. I saw her stand taller.

Her journey reminded me of the heavy spring snowfall we get here in Colorado, late in the spring, long into April and sometimes May. The tree branches have turned green with fresh leaves and buds, and suddenly they are weighed down with heavy, wet snow. The snow doesn't stay very long because the ground isn't cold enough to keep it there, but it weighs those branches all the way to the ground. If nobody sets them free, the branches break under the strain and the burden of that much snow.

We Coloradoans are out there on the morning after a snowfall, shaking the branches, using mops and broomsticks to reach as high as we can to wrestle the snow off the tree branches. I'm not ashamed to tell you that I even talk to the trees in my backyard. "Come on—you can do this. Stay with me," I'll say, as I reach near a trunk to shake its branches and set them free. With a good, strong shake, the snow falls to the ground, and the whole tree stands taller.

That is how it was with Tricia. This storm had weighed her down. What a sacred honor to reach into the cold mess, to find those branches fresh with life, to shake off the burden and watch her stand tall again.

Most of the suffering we see in the world is related to love and loss, and our role as therapists is to acknowledge, experience, and take on the reality of that love and loss, including its pleasure and heartbreak, what is good and bad about all that has happened. The only thing that makes it possible to do the ongoing labor of trauma work is the awe I feel at my patients' commitment to surviving. They endure dark nights of the soul, sometimes traveling them time and again, on the long path to recovery.

EIGHT

Walking Away

Tricia

For a while, I knew exactly how many days it had been since I talked to Annie. But then, like the breaking of any other addiction, days became weeks and months and years, until my brain and my nervous system and my emotional memory no longer needed to keep track.

I've learned since then that people keep track of those who have abused them for a lot of complicated, tangled reasons. People keep track out of hypervigilance, a sense that they'll be safer if they can keep tabs on where the abuser is and what they're up to. People keep track because our brains and nervous systems and emotional memories aren't black-and-white, and we feel both the harm and the grief of losing what once felt like good. But those things fade over time as our bodies and brains settle and distance allows the complex web of trauma and connection to feel less intense.

Trauma bonds are hard to break, and they don't break overnight. Becoming healthy looks like the slow fading of intense memories and emotions, the releasing of the need to reconnect, the laying down of hope that maybe, someday, the abuser will realize how harmful they were and will change.

Breaking my trauma bond with Annie didn't happen the instant I told her I was severing contact. One time I sent her a Facebook friend request, thinking maybe I could manage this friendship if it were only virtual and online. I thought maybe this was a measure of forgiveness, this step of letting her back into my life. But my newly steadied internal compass immediately went haywire, alerting me to the confusing breach of my own boundaries. I rescinded the request within the hour.

For a long, long time, I wondered if I had done the right thing in cutting her off. Maybe it's hard for anyone to walk away, and maybe it's even harder for a Christian to walk away. It just seems so final, so "no more chance." Could we really be sure this is what Jesus would do?

Jana said, "Think back in the Bible. When God closed the door of the ark, *he closed the door of the ark*.[1] He gave the people chances and warnings—boundaries, if you will. And then he closed the door, and the rain came down. He set the terms of relationship, and the people who didn't choose to follow him experienced the consequence of their choice."

She gave me another example. "Think of when Adam and Eve sinned in the Garden of Eden. They broke their relationship with God, and he sent them out of the Garden.[2] He didn't give them a time-out, and he didn't open it later to let them back in. He set the boundary, and he kept it."

And still, she gave me a third. "Think about Moses. He chose to act against what God had told him to do—and again, I think we can look at that as a significant boundary violation in their relationship. And the consequence was that Moses didn't get to go into the Promised Land."[3]

We talked about how in each of these examples God setting a boundary didn't mean the person didn't have a chance to repent. What it did mean, though, was that when the people broke relationship with God through their choices, he allowed them to experience the consequences of their behavior. Boundaries mean we are not allowing someone to continue sinning against us.

I want to be careful with the theology here, to not take these examples out of context and thereby say something not precisely correct about God. He does not turn away from people forever once they violate a boundary, and that's where the comparison breaks down.

God allows us to experience the consequences of sin and broken relationship, but he doesn't ever close us off forever from the possibility of repentance and reconciliation in this life. He's God, and that means he knows when heart change is true. That's why his boundary setting can more easily leave room for restoration of the relationship.

In contrast, based on our limited knowledge of the hearts

and minds of other people, we have to do it differently. We need to allow people to experience the consequences of their actions and then leave the restoration up to God. It's not our job to restore them or to fix the relationship. We get to trust that God has other ways of working in their lives.

Even still, I thought, those examples are all from the Old Testament. Isn't Jesus all about grace? This is what has always hung me up. I wanted an example of someone living under the covenant of grace who *still* said, "Enough." So I asked Jana, "Are there any examples in the New Testament, though?"

Jana thought about this, and then she said, "Well, there is the verse that says, 'Shake the dust off your feet.'⁴ Jesus gave the disciples explicit permission: *You don't have to come back to this town. If they don't receive what you have to say, you can move on. You can be done, absolutely.* Tricia, I do believe there are points when you can say, 'No more.'"

Could that really be true? Really?

In his book *When to Walk Away*, author and speaker Gary Thomas observes,

> Christians tend to think that walking away from anyone, or letting anyone walk away from the truth, is a failure on our part.
>
> But Jesus walked away or let others walk away . . . a *lot*.
>
> . . . *Sometimes to follow in the footsteps of Jesus is to walk away from others or to let them walk away from us.*⁵

In the Gospels, Jesus deliberately parted ways with people forty-one times. Jesus didn't walk away thoughtlessly, but he did walk away freely.[6]

I had to set down my pen and sit with that number. *Forty-one.*

But then, I thought, *If not me, who knew how deep the rot went—who was going to help Annie? Love her? Be "the church" to her?*

Gary Thomas provides some perspective on that, too:

I'm not a medical doctor. If someone has a broken arm, I can call a physician for them and show some empathy, but it would be irresponsible to think I could heal them. That kind of assistance is above my training and experience, and I'm likely to just make things worse if I get overly involved. When someone is a truly toxic individual, most of us normal people will be in over our heads. You can try all you want, but thinking you can be the one who breaks through is more likely to humble you than to change them.

You don't have to believe me; life alone will teach you, if you let it.[7]

More than that, I wasn't just some "normal person" who wanted to help some "truly toxic individual." My history with Annie was filled with harmful, distorted power dynamics. The layers of trauma and abuse meant that not only was I unqualified—I was unsafe. An abuse victim is the last person who should be put in the position of having to help their abuser. I needed to get safe and stay safe.

In the next week's session, I said to Jana, "So, I can keep the door closed. Is that what I am understanding correctly?"

She said, "You can keep the door closed. And I don't think you're ungodly to do so."

I said, "But who's going to help her?"

Jana leaned in closer to me, like she does when months of work are coming to a moment of clarity. She said, "Someone else may be able to open the door. But it's not yours to open."

She said, "God made us all different, with different skills, abilities, gifts, and boundaries. *We* have to be aware of ourselves, our personalities, to know how it affects us emotionally and what we are capable of carrying. It doesn't make us less, it doesn't make us mean, it doesn't make us less Christian. It doesn't make you a bad person to say, 'You are unhealthy in my life. I can no longer allow the things you have done.'"

"Then what is forgiveness?" I asked her.

Jana said, "Even if a person says, 'Please forgive me,' you do not have to step back into relationship with them. Forgiveness is not always reconciliation."

"That's the part I'm trying to figure out," I said.

I made a circle with my arms, like I was holding a bubble. I said, "I want to learn how to have compassion *from here*. I want to learn how to love *from here*. Compassion and love don't mean that I have to be the one to fix it, right? That has to be the bottom line, Jana. I can't be the one who has to fix it."

She winked at me. She has winked at me a handful of

times in our long years of work together. It's the wink of a job well done, of my self-discovery announcing itself in the sacred space between us.

"Tricia," she said, "you cannot fix it, you don't have to be the one to fix it, and it may not ever get fixed this side of heaven."

Jana

Stay with me here. I did say that, and I believe that it is true. History proves that some behaviors and some relationships will not be healed this side of heaven.

But can a person really change? Yes, I believe so, and my belief is based on a number of factors, grounded in both science and theology.

Perhaps you have heard of the Marshmallow Test, a remarkable experiment created by psychologist Walter Mischel. The scenario was simple. In the test, each child involved was presented with the opportunity to receive a marshmallow. Then the child was told that the researcher had to leave the room for a little while, but if the child could delay eating that first marshmallow until the researcher returned, the child could receive a second marshmallow.

Years later, Mischel and his colleagues followed up with some of their original Marshmallow Test participants, and their findings surprised the world. They found positive future outcomes among the children who had been able to delay gratification. Those individuals rated significantly higher on cognitive ability, they were better able to cope with stress and frustrations in adolescence, and they earned higher scores on the SAT. These correlations seemed to point to one conclusion: The ability to pass the Marshmallow Test was the key to a successful future.[8]

Our culture looked at the Marshmallow Test and concluded that our destiny—the trajectory of our personalities, our self-control, and our future—rests in our response to a marshmallow. That's the conclusion we drew, and that's what we have been telling ourselves and each other ever since.

But Mischel said that that couldn't be further from the truth. We misunderstood the whole thing.

It's possible that our culture skewed his test results to see what we wanted to see. Literally, the whole point of the original Marshmallow Test was to investigate and demonstrate how flexible people are, how easily they could change if given the opportunity to change perspective. In fact, Mischel and his colleagues discovered, people change all the time.

Most of the children in Mischel's test were able to delay gratification when they reframed the situation in front of them. The researchers tested the children and discovered, for example, that a little girl who would have immediately splurged on a marshmallow under ordinary circumstances was actually able to wait when given more information and the chance to reframe the situation before her. With just a little more information and motivation, the child could wait fifteen minutes or more. A small change could drastically change a person's behavior.[9]

In order to truly understand how people change, we must consider how personality and situation fit together with the mind. The mind houses every sort of unseen thing, including the beliefs, assumptions, and expectations that you've gathered over the course of your life. Your mind contains the accumulative result of your relationships with friends and family, as well as cultural expectations (what happens in the world around you).

Everything in your mind serves as the filter through which you see the world: how you respond to situations, whether patterned or unique. Your mind stands between who you are and whatever situation you are in, profoundly influencing how your brain interprets the world around it. Your mind affects what your brain sees in any situation and what it feels about what it sees.

When the stuff inside the mind changes, people change. They begin to interpret themselves, their lives, and their situations differently. They even begin to act different.

Mischel saw people as fundamentally flexible. He said that was the single most important thing he stood for in his entire professional life. He said,

> What my life has been about is in showing the potential for human beings to not be the victims of their biographies—not their biological biographies, not their social biographies—and to show, in great detail, the many ways in which people can change what they become and how they think.[10]

If we miss that part of the science, we miss the whole point of the study.

When we're talking about this kind of change, we're talking about movement away from the pull of our pasts and trauma, movement toward something more healed, more whole. Christians believe that movement doesn't happen from sheer force of will or because someone merely becomes more self-aware. It happens because there's another pull, a deeper truth about every single one of us that makes restoration not just possible but how life was meant to be.

Imago Dei is a Latin phrase that means "image of God." The Bible says all human beings are made in the image and likeness of God. How we carry that image may be blurred or obscured because of what we've gone through or the choices we make, but God's image is an inextricable part of who we are. The belief that every person has worth and dignity as an image bearer of God is an important overlapping element of theology and Christian counseling. Every person has human rights, and every person's life has value. Every person.

As a professional who seeks to serve God by helping heal wounds of the world, how do I practice the theology of *imago Dei*? I operate within this framework: Every person carries areas of brokenness, *and* every person can be changed, healed, and restored. In terms of human rights, this means that every person has value, regardless of race, gender, social status, and so on. It also means that every person has innate humanity and dignity—including those who perpetuate abuse.

Is it possible to look at one who is wounded and see hope for their healing? Yes.

Is it possible to look at one who wounds others and see hope for change? Yes.

I remind myself every day of my life: "With God all things are possible."[11] Because I believe this to be true, I ultimately believe that truly anything is possible.

If we do not own what we have done, if we hide our weaknesses, if we are outside healthy communication with godly people who can join us on a journey, if we are not willing to confront it and get the help, then our harmful behavior will continue. But if we humbly come before God, asking for guidance and wanting to improve our lives, then it can happen. If we are willing to own what we need to own, confess what we've done, and humble ourselves, he will help us—and he will guide us to people who can help with our healing.

Every single person can find restoration. No wound is too deep, and no person is too far down a path of abuse to find a new way. It is possible for anyone to change.

This cannot be overstated: An abusive person can own what they have done and choose to pursue restorative healing because anything is possible with God. Made in the image of God, every person is capable of moving toward becoming more whole.

So, then, I believe these statements to be true: Every person can change, and healthy people have boundaries. Wisdom says we should know our own limits in relationships with people who have not yet changed.

If we look at God's heart for people throughout the Bible—and remember, he is the same toward you and me—this is what we see: God's heart is always bent toward protecting the vulnerable and the oppressed. Psalm 10:14 (NIV) is only one of an abundance of verses in Scripture that talk about this:

> But you, God, see the trouble of the afflicted;
>   you consider their grief and take it in hand.
> The victims commit themselves to you;
>   you are the helper of the fatherless.

So, knowing that truth about God and holding it alongside how God models holding boundaries when people are acting in harmful ways, this is what I believe to be true:

- Abuse victims, the vulnerable and oppressed, are held by a loving Father who sees and grieves over every piece of their pain.

- Abusers, human beings who are also made in the image of God, obscure that image through how they carry it and grieve God by harming other image bearers.

- Only God can change a human heart.[12] We are not responsible for fixing someone else's sin or making them repent. God is the source of repentance and restoration.[13]

Establishing and maintaining boundaries with someone who has harmed you does not mean you think they are beyond God's reach, but it does mean that you are letting them experience the consequences of their sinful behavior. It means you are acknowledging that God can use means other than you to restore them.

Above all, I believe this is true: God honors the boundaries abuse victims hold against their abusers. We must not ask victims to take down a boundary that God himself may have put in place.

For Therapists

If you want to give your best to your people, you've got to set boundaries too. As a therapist, you may need to step back and evaluate whether your own triggers are influencing your therapeutic process with a client. Even a therapist has to set boundaries. Not every therapist can work with every client. You may have your own hurts that need healed.

Consider the process of jury selection for a court trial. The purpose of jury selection is to ensure that the jury is impartial, representing a fair cross section of the community. Potential jurors are questioned by the judge, prosecutors, and defense attorneys to determine whether they have any biases, prejudices, or personal conflicts of interest that would keep them from making a fair and impartial verdict. If a potential juror has a close relationship with the plaintiff or defendant or prior experience that would affect their judgment, they are dismissed from serving on the jury—sometimes without a reason stated.

Why is that? Because not everyone can help everybody. Sometimes our stories affect the way we seek and find justice, restoration, and healing.

Therapists, if you have extremely strong emotions related to a story a client brings, check yourself. You may need to float back in your memories to find your attachment. Decide carefully whether you are the best person to help. There is someone who can help that person. That someone might not be you—and, in fact, you might be a better help to that client by guiding them to a therapist who is a better fit.

NINE

Grieving

Tricia

"I can't risk it, Jana. If I'm going to heal, then I can't go near the one who broke me."

"I agree," she said.

"But I do miss her sometimes."

"Tell me about that," she said. "There must have been good moments, good people, and good feelings at some point. Tell me about those."

"Oh, man, Jana." I felt emotion welling in me. The grieving kind.

"Tell me," she said, her voice gentle and patient.

I closed my eyes. I could only think about Annie if I

closed my eyes. Jana said it was because I was stepping into those moments, recalling old experiences, and closing my eyes was the bridge from the present to that time, to Before. When I needed to step out of remembering, I could open my eyes and be present again. Closing my eyes gave me a sense of control.

I took a slow, deep breath. "I miss the good parts of life with her. I miss teaching with her. I really liked being with her. Is that okay?"

"That is okay. What else do you miss?"

"I miss thinking with her. She was a great thinker."

Jana asked, "Do you feel a tug-of-war with that statement?"

I opened my eyes. "Well, yes. I mean, she was a great thinker, yes. I imagine she still is. But she was also so good at manipulating things. She was playing the ultimate game of chess at all times."

"Yes, she was."

"So I didn't love that, no," I said.

I closed my eyes again. My voice came out as a whisper. "But I did love thinking with her. I loved thinking through things with her. There were gifts and abilities in me that she saw first. She was the first person to speak those out loud. She was the first person to recognize me as a teacher of adults. She was the first person to see me as a person with a pastor's heart."

Jana said, "Tell me about that."

"I remember Annie telling me that I was a pastor," I said, "and I disagreed with her. But she taught me that there are three general roles in ministry: a preacher, a pastor, and a priest. The preacher is the one who does the preaching and the teaching. The pastor is the one who holds your hand and goes through it with you. And the priest is the one who absolves the guilt of your sins. She said they're not always three separate roles, and they can spill over into one another, like a trinity of ministry. Three in one."

"Annie taught you that?"

"She did. She told me I was a pastor. She said I could see people, that I enter the mess with them and love them, and that's what a pastor does. I had never seen myself that way."

"And how do you feel about that now?" Jana asked.

My voice came out softer still. I was afraid to say it out loud. I whispered, "I don't want that to not be true about me."

Annie had taught me to love messy people. She'd challenged me to love them in a boundaryless way, with extravagant grace and generous love.

But then she *became* the messy person that I loved. She turned ministry into something that groped me in my sleep. And I no longer trusted myself to set a boundary because she had taught me that a pastor doesn't.

There was a lot that was good, until it wasn't.

I said, "There was a long list of things that were beautiful, until she misused them."

Jana clarified, "She abused you."

I was learning to use that word, fitting it into a long list of words I was learning to use.

Jana said, "Tricia, evil does its best work in the middle of good work. What she did to you was evil, and so very wrong. And it doesn't mean it didn't start out good. It doesn't mean that the good she saw in you hasn't been true all along."

We spent months working on the truth of that.

For a long time, my work in Jana's office consisted of her teaching me that there had been nothing wrong with me initially choosing to be friends with Annie.

What was wrong was that my friend had turned against me, betrayed me, and exploited me. Jana reminded me that the grief I felt in the aftermath was for the friend I had lost. Most of the time, I didn't feel sad about Annie because she gave me a lot to feel mad about instead. But sometimes the only word for my heart was *sad*. The healing would only happen as I let myself feel the sadness of so much that had been lost.

So I let myself feel the sadness as it exhaled into the space between my life and Annie's.

Jana

The decision to walk away is never easy. No matter how harmful or toxic the relationship, the things that kept us in it are the things that make it painful to leave.

Often people can't even pinpoint the breaking point, what pushed them to leave. There's not usually a moment of blinding, permanent clarity, because most of them have no idea what they were involved in until long after they get out from under it. That's the nature of psychological influence and manipulation. It takes time to realize what's going on, and walking away is a journey of disentangling and beginning our lives again with what we know now.

Nothing is ever only one thing. Every person, every

emotion, and every experience has layers upon layers—sometimes like an onion, sometimes like a rubber-band ball. You'll usually not be just sad or just angry. When you have one strong emotion, it's often attached to other strong emotions. Usually the strongest one is the one we can see and identify, so we grab on to it. But when we identify that strong emotion, as we peel it back, we can reveal other emotions that are quieter and softer. They're hidden. They might be difficult to identify or hard to admit.

Anger feels strong, but sadness feels painful. Grief, shame, guilt—any of those can push you back into a relationship. Undealt-with emotions will only entrap you more, subjecting you to many dangers. We will do anything to not feel sad.

I reminded Tricia to stand her ground. I told her, "Do not let your grief push you back into friendship with her, Tricia. Stay strong. Be cautious that you do not allow your grief to push you into a place you shouldn't be. The good that may have existed way back then is now darkened by the shadow of what Annie had in mind all along. You experienced very real betrayal, manipulation, and harm, and there is so much to grieve here. So let yourself grieve, and then let's look forward to the next part of your life."

Gary Thomas writes,

The church will save untold numbers of productive, joy-filled hours if we will learn to grieve our loss (which is healthy) instead of attempt to fix toxic relationships (which rarely, if ever, proves productive). Grieving usually leads to improved spiritual health and makes things better, at least for us as individuals. Attempting to bring function to dysfunction takes up a lot of time and usually makes things worse. *When we're dealing with toxicity, grieving is almost always better than fixing.*[1]

Grieving what is lost is one of the healthiest, most helpful things we can do, and it walks hand in hand with putting hard boundaries in place. Researcher and storyteller Brené Brown writes, "Those sharp edges feel vulnerable, but they are also the markers that let us know where we end and others begin."[2]

TEN

Naming What Happened

Tricia

Madeleine L'Engle says that writing is very much like praying: Both involve discipline; both involve listening. If the artist only writes when they know what to say, they are far less apt to find clarity and inspiration, since those often show up once the artist gets to work. In the same way, if I only pray when I know what to say, I may never hear God's answer. He may never choose to speak. Madeleine says, "The greatest moments of prayer come in the midst of fumbling and faltering prayer."[1]

Jana had given me homework: to write down what had happened. (Not all therapists would call it "homework," but she knows I'm a perpetual student. Homework is a language I understand.) I couldn't recall a time when I had so equally wanted and not wanted to write. I didn't know what to say. I found myself delaying with absurdities—trimming my fingernails, my sons' fingernails, or anyone's fingernails.

When I tried to write, my pen dried up.

Not literally; the pen worked fine. And, in any case, I always have a dozen pens in my bag.

But my words ran away. My handwriting changed.

Writing has always demanded much of me: truth, bravery, patience, and the willingness to follow my own words, whether they slog up one hill or race down another. The pen and the page have become my most fundamental spiritual practice, my most essential path of worship. That is not to say that writing is my only prayer, nor that everything I write is a prayer. But I will say that the two usually happen at the same time, and it is always worship.

Writing this story would require grief, rage, humility, failure, grace, and forgiveness. It would be a study of toxic relationships, of secrets and accountability, of shame and vulnerability. It would be freedom for me, and for others. I know I am not the only one, not even the only one to be victimized by this particular abuser. Writing this story would be the greatest offering of all.

I don't know whether I let myself begin or I made myself begin, but finally, I began.

I let myself write whatever came to my mind, recording

every memory as it bubbled up in a stream of free writing. An image brought a memory, and a memory brought a paragraph. I wrote them down.

I started studying story, how to tell it as concisely as possible. I knew that every story has three parts: a beginning, a middle, and an end. With further study, I learned it can be as brief as three lines, if they contain all the three parts of a fairy tale.

In the beginning, something happened so that a person had a problem and a need.

As the person pursued his or her desire, a struggle ensued.

And in the end, the person changed with a realization.[2]

Here is one of my stories, frankly the safer of the two:

Once upon a time, there was a woman whose husband died very suddenly, two days before Christmas, leaving her a widowed single mother of two boys not yet in kindergarten.

As the woman tried to put her life back together, she wrestled with the deepest questions of sovereignty and faith, all through the dark veil of panic, anxiety, PTSD, and deep depression.

In the end, the woman emerged from two years of winter in her soul, now with a tangible understanding of the presence of God in the darkest night, a knowledge of Scripture as a path of honest prayer, and a recognition that she was fiercely powerful and profoundly fearless.

But also, this is my story:

Once upon a time, there was a woman whose friend was a habitual abuser, and the woman became the abuser's target.

As the woman tried to be a good friend, the lines blurred, and the abuser caused the woman to question everything she understood about her boundaries, identity, intellect, spirituality, sexuality, and intuition. The woman was caught in a web of lies and manipulation and became a keeper of the abuser's secrets. When the woman became a widow, the abuser trapped her in ongoing abusive patterns, and the widow did not understand how to free herself from the cultlike influence of someone she had trusted.

In the end, the widow discovered she had been targeted, manipulated, isolated, and abused. She set a solid boundary, permanently severing every tie to the abuser. The widow discovered anew who she was, what she truly wanted, and that her boundaries, her intuition, and her voice could be trusted.

I brought the words to Jana, the fragments and pieces, the parts of the whole. Sometimes I read them aloud, sometimes I just showed her that I had done what she'd asked me to do.

For a while, I really wanted Jana to name Annie as a narcissist or a sociopath. As long as naming things gives us power, let's give Annie a name too.

But Jana was insistent: "She's not my patient, Tricia. You are. I am not diagnosing her."

Fair enough, legal licensing and all such things considered.

I learned that my healing and my story had to be independent of anything Annie is ever named, accused of, found guilty of, or recovering from. In knowing and telling the truth, I had to let go of any other outcome, including investigations, verdicts, and perceptions. Those are not a measure of the truth, and they are not a part of my story.

My story is seeing clearly. My story is the choice to heal. My story is the ending I am writing, the beginning of my freedom.

Jana

One of the most formidable and empowering actions you can take is giving a name to what happened to you. We think that naming something gives it power, but in reality, naming something removes its power and transfers that power to you. It's tempting to talk about trauma as an abstract thing, but healing comes in facing what is true. This happens as we learn to talk about it. Naming something gives you authority.

"God is also honored when we call things by their right name," says Dr. Diane Langberg. "Clergy sexual abuse is *not* an affair; pedophilia is not about struggling with difficult circumstances; molesting adolescents is not about a struggling marriage. Such things need to be called by their right names, and the abusive person needs to be held responsible for his/her abusive behavior."[3]

Being Known is a podcast hosted by Dr. Curt Thompson, a psychiatrist and author who focuses on the intersection of neuroscience, spirituality, and relationships. He and cohost Pepper Sweeney have released a series of brilliant dialogues about trauma; how it affects the mind, body, and brain; and the healing power of telling your story to find wholeness. Here are some helpful insights from them about naming what happened:

- The enemy's best work "depends on us not naming what is true." He is the Ultimate Deceiver, and he will tell you lies until you tell them to yourself. He wants you to believe either that your trauma is too small to mention or that your trauma is too big to heal. If you think either of those extremes is true, then you won't give a name to the harm you experienced.[4]

- When you can name what happened to you, you can get help. When you get help, you are seen, known, and honored in your pain. Shame no longer gets to run the show. In the process of knowing and being known is when trauma can be identified, healed, and even brought to fullness and beauty.[5] As Ann Voskamp says, "Shame dies when stories are told in safe places."[6]

- Learning your story can help you understand why you do the things you do. Curt Thompson says, "If I asked you to pick up a fifty-pound boulder, probably you could do it. If I asked you to carry it for a ten-mile hike through the Colorado mountains, you'd get maybe one hundred yards in before you'd start shifting the weight of the rock, trying to find a new way to carry it. Soon you'd want to set it down. But life doesn't always let us set things down, so we have to find new ways to carry the heavy things. These are called *coping mechanisms*. It's how we learn to survive. Without therapy and healing, we reinforce our trauma with our coping mechanisms."[7]

If you are stuck in a behavior that confuses you, it might be a coping mechanism that you established because you've been carrying heavy things for a long, long time.

Trauma is very difficult to articulate because organizing a traumatic experience into a coherent account is an enormously difficult task. We probably don't remember trauma as a story with a beginning, middle, and end. As is consistent with complex trauma, the details knot themselves into isolated images without any context, other than fear and panic. As you begin to sort through the details of your story, though, you give language to your anger, sadness, and confusion. And that's a good thing—those nameless emotions have been waiting for a long time to speak.

Anger is one of the first signs of recovery, and it's also the most difficult emotion for many people to get in touch with. Anger is a normal, appropriate reaction to the hurt you've experienced. If you feel angry as you organize the details of your story, it means you've had time to sit with the ways you've been wronged and you're ready to acknowledge that you've been victimized. What happened to you may have been damaging, destructive, and even devastating. You are entitled to get angry.

As people learn to talk about what happened to them, they may settle into a script or a sound bite for public consumption, and that's entirely fair. The script creates some distance from the incoherent details and overwhelming emotions, enabling a person to acknowledge the facts of what happened without reliving the trauma every time.

When I encouraged Tricia to write her story out, it took a while for her to even get out her pen. That should tell us something about the depth of the trauma—when even Tricia doesn't want to write about it. Still, I pressed her on this one. Not just because she's a writer but because writing is good therapy. When you write to yourself, you don't need to worry about what other people think. You simply listen to your thoughts and write them down. Later, when you read what you've written, you might discover surprising truths. Writing is excellent therapy.

You might cry as you write, and that's okay too. Once again, to quote Curt Thompson, "You're worried that if you start to weep, you'll never stop. And [I] say, [I] want you to weep until you're done. . . . Your tears are telling [you] something about what your heart needs the world to know."[8]

ELEVEN

Healing Body, Mind, and Heart

Tricia

Trauma rushes through every part of us, hiding in corners of our minds and bodies until suddenly, there it is, a reaction, a panic attack, an overwhelming emotion rising to the surface. Because trauma leaves markers along every path in our very selves—brain, body, spirit, emotions, relationships, and beyond—the healing from trauma necessarily requires healing along many pathways.

For me, Jana said my next pathway toward healing would involve learning to be touched again.

This seemed like something a person should be able to

do, right? I've always been a hugger. Widowed or not, surely I hadn't forgotten how to touch people.

She clarified the difference: Physical self-awareness is an essential step in finding freedom from this kind of wound. The mind needs to be reeducated to feel physical sensations, and the body needs to enjoy the comfort of safe touch.

Touching another person wasn't the task. The task was learning *to be touched.*

I shrank back when she said that. Yep, there was a difference between touching and being touched. One I could control. The other was where control had been taken from me. Already I didn't like it.

She explained that a person can't fully recover without feeling safe in their skin,[1] and yet traumatized people are afraid of feeling. The perpetrator is no longer a danger to us; our own physical sensations have become the enemy. People don't realize how consuming this can be, when each physical sense is an entry point for trauma. A lot of traumatized people become compulsive at numbing: We overeat and compulsively drink, we fear any intimacy, and we avoid social activities, all because our sensory world is off-limits.

We might simultaneously crave touch and feel terrified of body contact, but we can only become immune to triggers when we become aware of what triggers us. For me, that would require letting down my guard with physical touch.

Triggered responses show up in lots of ways, sometimes in response to the slightest cue. A flashback to the trauma, a horrifying reliving of the event that feels like it could go on forever, can occur at any time. So a lot of traumatized people structure their lives around trying to protect against flashbacks, and this safeguard often includes keeping other people from touching us.

Jana explained that safety and terror are incompatible. They can't exist in the same place at the same time. To be emotionally close to another human being (which I hoped I would someday be able to do), we must learn how to be physically close to others. That means our defensive systems must temporarily shut down. The brain has to turn off its vigilant state. In healthy physical intimacy, a person can be still without feeling afraid.

I couldn't do that. I didn't know how anymore.

My homework that week: to make an appointment with a massage therapist.

No can do, Jana.

I returned the following week without doing the homework. That happened a few times, over several weeks. As always, Jana was patient. She waited, and then one day I did it. I made the appointment.

I used to see massages as indulgent forms of self-care, right up there with manicures and bougie lattes (both of which I also enjoy, thank you very much). The fluffy robe, the ethereal music, the lit candles, and the citrus lotions. Aside from the trauma of it all, I could get on board with this prescription.

As I lay on the table, covered in layers of fresh linen sheets, the massage therapist began to massage my scalp. And I began to cry. I didn't know why, but there were a lot of tears that day. Tears of everything.

I read later,

> Just like you can thirst for water, you can thirst
> for touch. It is a comfort to be met confidently,
> deeply, firmly, gently, responsively. Mindful touch
> and movement grounds people and allows them to
> discover tensions that they may have held for so long
> that they are no longer even aware of them. When
> you are touched, you wake up to the part of your
> body that is being touched.[2]

Perhaps I was crying because I was waking up.

Since my husband had died, when had I last been touched *at all*? When had I been touched by someone who wasn't asking to be touched in return? Without harm or shame?

Physical touch makes it possible for a person to live in their body. You might not even know it's an ability you've lost until you get it back. That was certainly true of me. People who live in fear need to learn a sense of where their bodies are, and they need to feel a sense of safe boundaries. Bodywork and massage therapy let a person do this; firm, reassuring touch lets them know what is outside them, where their bodies end.

When we can feel our bodies, we can feel our boundaries.

If safety and terror cancel one another out, if trust and relaxation are directly linked, then this "learning to relax" would take some time. I proceeded with many appointments with my massage therapist, who was as masterful with her hands and pressure as Jana was with her questions and silences.

As I sought relaxation, I couldn't always predict my responses. A particular touch might bring up anger, fear, grief, or another powerful emotion that surprised me. Sometimes I reacted with a strong physical response, cringing or trembling. Sometimes I knew what was causing this response, and other times I couldn't name why I felt or reacted this way. But my body knew things that my memory couldn't recall. I carried troubling stories and memories in my muscles, in my bones, and in the cells of my body.

That's when I began to understand that the mind and the body are connected.

To find freedom in either one, healing had to happen along both paths.

To explore one of the more magical pathways toward healing the mind, let's imagine for a minute that my brain is a giant warehouse with two halves, a left half and a right half. The left half of the brain warehouse files away facts, statistics, and vocabulary words; experiences, dates, and details. I count on the left side to recall things that happened in the correct order.[3]

The right side of the warehouse stores intuition, feelings, visual experiences, and spatial and tactual events, as well as memories of sound, touch, smell, and emotions. This part of the warehouse processes and reacts to voice inflection, facial features, gestures, and places.[4] The things in this area of the warehouse could be called intuitive truth: They feel like facts to me, like the way things are, but someone else could perceive them differently.

On each side of the warehouse are rows, aisles, and stacks of filing cabinets, all connected on neuropathways that dip and swirl like a winding conveyor belt that looks like a roller coaster. All my thoughts, experiences, and new memories show up as items on a conveyor belt, a machine that I imagine operates sort of like a bowling-ball retriever. As things pop up, my brain knows exactly where to file the new information, since under ordinary circumstances, the two sides of the brain work together smoothly. Your brain works this way too.

Now, what this means is that when I suddenly feel afraid, that emotion pops up on the conveyor belt. My brain zips that feeling away to the file of other things that are dangerous: snakes, slamming on the brakes, touching a hot stove, walking near the edge of a cliff. Whenever something new makes me feel afraid, my brain says, *Yes. We know this feeling. We've got to guard against this thing now too. To keep her safe, we must file this feeling in the dangerous file.*

When I accidentally send my son to school without a permission slip on a field-trip day, my brain puts that experience away with other experiences that were my fault: I missed a writing deadline, drove over the speed limit, forgot a meeting. The next time something is my fault, my brain knows what to do: *Aha. This goes in the Feel Guilty file.*

But things get tricky when files get misplaced. When technically a piece of information could go in more than one file and spins off in the wrong direction in the brain.

My husband died on my watch. He was gone before the paramedics arrived. It wasn't my fault, but my brain didn't know that.

I feel shame for what Annie did to me, even though she was an abuser with a calculated plan, script, and steps to follow. It wasn't my fault, but my brain didn't know that.

Each of these misplaced files pops up on the conveyor belt, and my brain recognizes them without processing them. My brain sees fear, guilt, and shame, so it follows the well-worn path to those filing cabinets and files each of these where it thinks they belong.

But they don't fit there. They get stuck before the drawer closes, and they clog the system.

New information, memories, and experiences pop up on the conveyor belt, but now my brain doesn't even know what to do, where to send anything, because it no longer trusts the process. New sensations come to the surface, but they activate my alarm system, which causes me to react as if I were back in my bedroom, watching my husband die. Or back being violated without my consent. The passage of time is erased. The heart rate increases. The blood pressure elevates. The gears shut down, and the conveyor belt in the brain warehouse stops running.

When anything happens that reminds a traumatized person of something dangerous in the past, their right brain reacts as if the traumatic event were happening in this very moment, as if the danger were present all over again. The memory is stuck. Their left brain doesn't respond accurately, so they may not even recognize that this reaction is illogical. They just feel mad, afraid, embarrassed, or paralyzed with anger.[5]

Suddenly I can't concentrate on the book I'm reading,

though I've read the paragraph three times. Or I feel over-whelmed by the sheer decibel volume of dinner conversation. I can't make decisions at the grocery store. I get headaches that feel like I've been hit in the face with a softball.

Sometimes this happens many times a day. That is, until I start the work of EMDR (Eye Movement Desensitization and Reprocessing) therapy.

A round of EMDR may require dozens of sessions over the course of many weeks or even months. EMDR is slow work, the rewiring of the brain, a fixing of the gears and conveyor belt and reorganizing of the files.

I "mood dress" for the work of EMDR: yoga pants and a long sweater, all black with a brightly colored scarf. Comfortable, colorful, and confident, reminding myself that I can do this, that it's like facing a difficult but life-saving medical procedure—because that's exactly what it is.

The therapy of EMDR involves tools that activate the different halves of the brain so memories can be rewired. I choose vibrating pulsers I can hold in my hands. This is where EMDR gets strange and a bit magical. As Jana and I talk, the vibrations cross the hemispheres between the left and right sides of my brain, and some way, somehow, that helps with the rewiring. Some people wear headphones for EMDR, but I don't because they make me feel like I'll miss something. Jana says that that's a sign of the hypervigilance, a sign of how I still can't let down my guard. Everything affects everything.

I sit in the chair in Jana's office, comfortable under a weighted blanket. She checks the pulsers; I confirm that the speed and intensity are right. I close my eyes, and she tells me to start whenever I'm ready.

There's something surprisingly comforting about the peaceful rhythm of the vibration, back and forth, back and forth. It feels like someone flickers the lights in the warehouse of my brain, reminding the roller coaster of conveyor belts that it was once a well-oiled machine. The gears turn, waking up. That's when Jana prompts me to go to a memory.

The best way I can explain this is that I step into the basement of my memories. I go down a flight of stairs and realize it's all there. Every memory, even the ones I think I've forgotten, the ones I didn't know I ever knew.

The practice of EMDR doesn't necessarily start out with the hard, scary, traumatizing memories. The therapy may work up to that, gently helping the brain remember how it works, how to get back on track. When we do move into the trauma memories, Jana is there with me, and I'm ready. Generally, the rational brain can override the emotional brain, as long as fear doesn't hijack the whole process. As long as I can keep one foot in the present, I can revisit a memory without feeling retraumatized by it. I see the memory, but I don't have to live it again. I can watch it without getting hurt by it. I can be the narrator of the story, not the victim of it. I might say "she" instead of "I."

Jana watches carefully, making sure I don't slip too far into remembering. Too far where I forget that it's not happening here and now. The moment I begin to feel trapped or afraid, then I'm vulnerable to falling into old patterns and following their directions. We are here to create a new neuropathway, so she talks to me while I revisit the memory, keeping me anchored to the present with her voice. She reminds me to take slow, deep breaths, to stay in the parasympathetic state. She says things like "Notice that" and "What happens next?" and "Where do you feel that right now?"

As I revisit the memory and tell the story, as I answer Jana's questions, I learn how to own my emotional brain again. I learn how to observe the memories of things that have happened to me, how to revisit the events and tolerate them, how to feel the gut-wrenching sensations that register as shame and humiliation. A person can tolerate a great deal of discomfort as long as we understand that it's fleeting. This isn't forever; it's only now. Even better, it was then. I'm only revisiting it. And as I confront what happened to me, the science of EMDR creates a new neuropathway from the left to the right side of my brain.

In my imagination, the right side of my brain starts to shine with a light that gets my attention. It seems to say, *Look over here. There's a new path. The memories don't have to get stuck where they don't fit. They just need a new place to live. Look on this side. There are files over there, and they have better names. "Not your fault." "Freedom." "Safe."*

For a while, all I can do is see that they could live somewhere else. I can't put them there yet because this session is over.

Jana calls me up from the basement of my mind. She has me touch each fingertip to my thumb, take off my shoes, and feel my toes against the carpet. She has me do real things with my actual body, to remind me that the memory lives in the past and I live in this moment. She brings me back, making sure I'm solidly present in my life, in my mind, and in my body. And we call it a day.

One week later, we do the whole thing again.

And a week later, we do it again.

And a week later, we do it again.

Every time the memory appears on the conveyor belt, EMDR shines the light to the new neuropathway. For months, it can feel like nothing is happening. The brain is strong in what it thinks it knows, and it does what it does. It's really hard to move a memory from one file to another.

And then, one day, I am out living my life in my actual world, and I see someone wearing an Ohio State jersey. My husband Robb's favorite team. I am flooded with the memory of his face as he died, of that moment when I couldn't save him.

The memory is the same, but this time it's also different. Somehow, it makes a bubble-popping sound, like the packing materials that come in shipping boxes. *Pop.*

Yes, he died. But it wasn't my fault.

Yes, he died, but my children are not at risk.

Yes, he died, but that doesn't mean everyone I love is at risk.

And that is how I know that the memory found a new place to live in my brain, the file where it always belonged.

Healing from trauma is much more than telling a story about something that happened long ago. Telling a story doesn't change how you feel about it. But when you can understand why you feel a certain way, then it's not so overwhelming. When you have the power to respond, to eat and sleep and conduct your life the way you want to, that's when the fire-breathing dragon loses the fight.

Jana and I have done this trauma work many times, focusing on the deepest images that were stuck, the memories that needed to be reprocessed and filed in a truer, more suitable place. We have reprocessed the moment that Robb died. But we have also reprocessed the cluster of experiences connected to Annie, the ongoing progressions of many memories associated with grooming, psychological abuse, and manipulation. There are more negative cognitions with something so complex, as opposed to a single episode. It has taken a long, long time.

You might be reading this and thinking, *Well, that hardly sounds worth the price of admission. That sounds awful.*

I'll agree. There's a special tension between living in the pain and confronting the healing. Healing is hard work. But the alternative is worse. When you can activate your gut feelings instead of avoiding them, when you can listen to your heartbreak instead of silencing it, and when you can make new, kinder pathways for yourself—things begin to change.

I am here to tell you: I can talk about it now. And being able to talk about it has unfolded even more pathways of compassion, acceptance, and ever-increasing healing.

Seven years after I learned to drink coffee, I became a barista at Starbucks. After writing at the corner table for so many hours straight that even my laptop smelled like coffee beans,

I finally donned my own green apron and joined the baristas behind the counter. Oh, the irony of acquired tastes.

Robb had been gone for five years. My little boys had grown into bigger boys but not quite yet young men. They were without a dad, and I was without a whole lot of things, when I picked up a Tuesday-evening shift and poured a latte for a handsome man who would change my life forever.***

Before I tell this story, hear me well: A person deserves healing because a person deserves healing. I don't want to imply for a fraction of a moment that a person who has been traumatized only deserves to find healing so they can find love, even love the second time around. Healing is not ever about your future with anybody else. You have the rest of your life to spend with yourself, and you deserve to be well and whole. That is a complete thought, sentence, and whole love story in itself.

I'm including the part about the latte and the love story, and I'm introducing you to my husband, Peter, because his presence in my life introduced a whole new series of wounds that needed tending, highlighting a whole new pathway into healing.

Learning to trust other people is probably the single most important aspect of mental health. And it's at the root of the profound human longing for intimacy. Intimacy—knowing and being known—is all we ever want, I think, and it carries the inherent qualities of longing, creativity, and vulnerability. Intimacy is fragility and power combined,

***For the full story, see other books I've written: *You Can Do This* and *Just. You. Wait.*

so it must be respected, protected, and entered into with eyes wide open.

Whatever form trust and intimacy take after trauma, these things are a sign of the hard work you've done and more hard work ahead. That's why I'm telling this story here.

For me, the hard work of mind and body healing allowed me to start a healthy relationship, but it also started me down a new pathway surrounding sexual trauma. Sexual trauma, after all, keeps hurting long after it is over.

I told Peter all about Annie. He had a lot of questions. I answered many of them, Jana answered others, and our marriage counselor helped us find answers to even more. (Brave couples see therapists.)

Like all the best people in my life, my husband is present in the slow measures of kindness. He doesn't mind when I have to touch his face while he's sleeping to make sure he's still here. He has learned, both intuitively and intentionally, how to navigate the layers and triggers of complex trauma. He is intentional to walk alongside me without making my burden his baggage. We each have a therapist, and we both know our triggers and own our stuff. And when either of us does our work, we both find healing. These are not small things.

There's a lot about each of our stories that Peter and I would not have chosen. But each day, we heal together as we choose each other. In the home we have made, we have these words on display:

When you recognize that you will thrive not in spite of your losses and sorrows, but because of them, that you would not have chosen the things that happened in your life, but you are grateful for them, that you will hold the empty bowls eternally in your hands, but you also have the capacity to fill them? The word for that is *healing*.[6]

Jana

When Tricia first came to me, I had been studying for years under two leading experts in the field of trauma work: Bessel van der Kolk, a world-renowned expert in EMDR, and Barb Maiberger, an experienced EMDR practitioner with a private practice in Colorado. With extensive practice and training, I earned my certification in EMDR, a therapy that helps people find relief from pain caused by traumatic events in their past.

I entered the science carefully and even skeptically, with deep respect for the fact that EMDR isn't right for everyone. Accessing old trauma can be very upsetting, and a poorly trained therapist—one who will skip steps or fail to complete sessions—can cause further harm to a traumatized person. Though I am certified as an EMDR therapist, I do not recommend it to all my clients, and I did not recommend this mode of therapy to Tricia for several years. We had to verbally dissect her two traumas into separate traumas before we could incorporate body-centered principles in her healing.

People have found freedom and healing through EMDR, even those who have long been burdened with trauma that they could not even name or remember. As Barb Maiberger says, "EMDR is not magic, but when it works, the relief is so great that it often feels magical."[7]

After several years of therapy and with careful assessment, I believed Tricia was an excellent candidate for EMDR therapy. Her progress as well as her commitment to healing had brought her to a place where EMDR was the best next step.

The therapy of EMDR is based on the premise that the brain inherently knows how to heal on its own, given the opportunity to properly store information. We store information in the form of memories, but sometimes an event gets locked into our brain. For some reason, that event cannot become a normally processed memory. When it gets stuck, it can create emotional disturbances that cause trauma symptoms.

Trauma work is designed to help you process a traumatic memory that you couldn't process as it happened, for any reason that may have been. Perhaps it was too overwhelming at the time, there was too much going on, you were too young, you didn't have the support you needed, you were sedated, or as a habit you tend to push things away that seem painful. When a memory cannot be processed, emotions from the past begin to feel like they're happening in the present. We need to help that memory find its way along the path to the past.

Healing depends on letting ourselves experience what the body already knows to be true, but we spend a lot of time separating our thoughts from what the body knows. Most people who experience trauma become so upset when they think about what they experienced that they try to push it out of their minds, acting as if it never happened. This requires tremendous energy, separating the mind and body.

The part of our brains designed to safeguard our survival is not very good at denial. So, in trying to act as if nothing happened, the brain acts as if the threat is still in the present. The body continues to defend against a threat that belongs in the past.

Healing requires and includes new neural formation—not just reintegrating old things but also making new connections and allowing ourselves to know and understand what is going on with us while we process the memories of the trauma. This is how we heal from trauma.

After all, you need to feel free to know what you know and feel what you feel, without any baggage attached. To know something isn't wrong. To feel a feeling isn't shameful. It is difficult enough to face what someone has done to you, but on a deeper level, a traumatized person is often even more troubled because of the shame they feel from what they did or did not do when they were being abused. When a person is made to feel anger, shame, or overwhelm because of their knowledge and emotions, they may begin to hide what they knew or felt in the face of their own trauma. But, as the prophet Jeremiah wrote, "you can't heal a wound by saying it's not there."[8]

The EMDR process allows the patient to access thoughts, images, emotions, and sensations related to the trauma while the left and right sides of the brain are externally stimulated in an alternating sequence. Those are fancy words that mean you're engaging your left and right side, back and forth. Left, right. Left, right. Left, right. Original EMDR research included eye movement, glancing back and forth from left to right, but now the therapy also allows for headphones with tones in the left ear and then the right or pulsers to hold in the hands as they gently vibrate, alternating between left and right.

The speed and stimulation can be varied, depending on what feels comfortable to the patient. Once the therapist and patient have established a bilateral rhythm that is comfortable, the memories can be revisited. The therapist guides the patient in the remembering, with intentional questions to help the patient recognize how they felt in that moment, how they feel now recalling that memory, where they feel it in their body, and other times when they have felt this sensation. When we can connect these physical sensations to the memory, when we can replace the cognition with what is true now, then we can help the brain process the memory and integrate it in the place where it belongs.

When traumatic memories have been processed, when everything in your system is working efficiently, then your brain can take in information, sort it accurately, and process it into long-term memory. You will remember the traumatic event, and you will have a story to tell about it, but it won't carry an emotional charge that shocks you every time. You may never like what happened, but you will be able to remember it and eventually even talk about it without falling apart. We will not erase the memory, but we will change your relationship to the memory. It will become *just a memory*, rather than a fire-breathing dragon that controls your life.

It is science, not magic. But indeed: The relief is so great that the science feels like magic.

TWELVE

Forgiving

Tricia

I lie awake at night, thinking about forgiveness, what it is and what it is not, this daily practice of opening my hands. And then, perhaps because I am watching for them, conversations and lessons about forgiveness start to appear all around me. Like when you look at the sky on a clear night, and the longer you sit still and stare, the more stars you see.

I am beginning to learn that guilt, shame, forgiveness, and compassion are all characters in the same story, and each one takes time to explore. If any single one of them is rushed or misunderstood, the story can go in the wrong direction.

Guilt plays a role, yes, as it may help you avoid making the same mistake twice, but excessive guilt prevents you from growing and learning from your mistakes.

Shame needs to be called out for what it is, or else it cripples a person's self-esteem and halts their emotional healing. It's the worst villain of all, the silencer of stories.

Forgiveness is one of the heroes, conquering shame and guilt. Often the first step toward forgiveness is forgiving yourself. This starts as you become clear about who you were when you got involved in this controlling relationship.

That's where compassion comes in. Above all, have compassion for yourself, and remember, being susceptible to the influence of another person is not the same as being culpable or complicit in their behavior.[1]

Each of these characters emerges in my thoughts on a daily basis. They're each still playing their roles. On my healthiest, most compassionate days, I choose forgiveness.

Counselor and author John Eldredge writes:

> Forgiveness is a choice. It not a feeling, but an act of the will. . . . We acknowledge that [what someone said or did] hurt, that it mattered, and we choose to extend forgiveness to [the person who wronged us]. This is *not* saying, "It didn't really matter"; it is *not* saying, "I probably deserved part of it anyway." Forgiveness says, "It was wrong, it mattered, and I release you."[2]

Forgiveness and release—these things take time. And they don't always result in reconciliation.

Kelly Corrigan is one of my favorite authors and storytellers. She proposes at least three choices in the multiple-choice manual of life: (a) forgive, (b) forgive and forget, or (c) forgive and separate.[3] *Forgive* on its own is a releasing, a moving forward, choosing to be in relationship while at the same time being cautious and aware, knowing that the other person has not necessarily owned their behavior. *Forgive and forget* is a choice to say, "This issue is not heavy or harmful enough over the long term to impact our relationship," believing that repentance has made space for reconciliation. But *forgive and separate* means we can forgive someone and walk away from the relationship, the very same day. This happens when staying in relationship means allowing the other person to continue to sin against us. It means they not only do not own their harm but also are intent on continuing the harm. Forgiving this person means releasing our anger while at the same time allowing them to experience the consequences of broken relationship. Holding our boundaries and forgiving someone can happen at the same time.

I've also reflected on how forgiveness must be turned inward to be lived outward. Healing from abuse is a long journey of now-me wondering how then-me could have let this happen. "Hindsight is 20/20" is a cliché for a reason, and it is exponentially true when your hindsight involves the layers of psychological entrapment and abuse. *If I had just told someone earlier. If I had just said no more loudly. If I had just, if I had just, if I had just . . .*

Poet and activist Maya Angelou said,

It's one of the greatest gifts you can give to yourself.
Forgive. Forgive everybody. Just forgive it. . . . So
then, you forgive, and it *relieves* you. You are *relieved*
of carrying that burden of resentment. You really are
lighter. You feel lighter—you just drop that. Then
you're free to do other things, to have some ambition
and so forth. . . .[4]

Forgive yourself for every failure. Because you tried
to do the right thing—God knows that, and you
know it. Nobody else may know it. . . .[5]

In Dr. Angelou's conversation with Oprah Winfrey,
Oprah responds with the now-famous axiom, "If you had
known better, you would have done better."

And then Dr. Angelou says, "Of course you would." And
then I raise my coffee cup. Yes. Of course I would.

Over the many years since I cut off contact with Annie,
the danger and power of Annie have faded, but other enemies linger. These are the enemies that can keep me trapped,
hemmed in, stuck in a defensive posture, that try to cut me
off from the freedom of forgiveness.

Brené Brown once told Father Richard Rohr that she
sometimes changes the words to familiar prayers and verses
to make them her own, to let her feel closer to God as she
prays. For example, when praying the Lord's Prayer, instead

of praying *Deliver us from evil*, she prays, *Deliver us from fear and shame.*[6]

When I read about David praying for protection from his enemies in Psalm 59, I think about Brené's words. I don't have the kinds of enemies David did, and I praise God for that. May it always be so. But fear and shame are real, relentless, evil, the opposite of the love of God. They are my enemies.

So I rewrote the psalm, making it a prayer of my own, replacing the word *enemies* with *fear and shame*.

Rescue me from [fear and shame], O God.
>   Protect me from those who have come to destroy me.
Rescue me from [fear];
>   save me from [shame].
They have set an ambush for me. . . .

They come out at night,
>   snarling like vicious dogs
>   as they prowl the streets.
Listen to the filth that comes from their mouths;
>   their words cut like swords. . . .

But as for me, I will sing about your power.
>   Each morning I will sing with joy about your
>   unfailing love.
For you have been my refuge,
>   a place of safety when I am in distress.
>   [Destroy fear and shame, my God. Wipe them out
>   completely.]

O my Strength, to you I sing praises,
    for you, O God, are my refuge,
    [No shame can live here.]
    the God who shows me unfailing love.

PSALM 59:1-3, 6-7, 16-17

I pray these words often: *Rescue me from fear and shame.*

This is how I begin to forgive myself. And as I do, my forgiveness moves outward in ways that are deeper, more true, more lasting. When fear takes a back seat, I am centered and calm, able to step back and see myself and my story more clearly. When shame isn't driving, I don't feel guilty about forgiving with no intent for reconciliation. I can hold in tension the good with the terrible, knowing both that the harm can be forgiven and that, for my own health and safety, any good does not cancel out that harm.

As my forgiveness becomes openhanded, it becomes less about Annie and more about the wide expanse of goodness in front of me. Over and over, I release that part of my story to the hands of God. And I step into the freedom ahead.

Jana

We think *forgiveness* means *justice*, but it might not mean that.

Forgiveness and justice are two different things, and healing is yet a third.

Like emotions, forgiveness happens in layers and stages.

Forgiveness does not have to mean forgetting.

Forgiveness does not require putting yourself back in harm's way.

Forgiveness is not always reconciliation.

You can forgive in your heart and not have to interact with the abuser. Period. Done. Mic drop.

Becoming Free

Tricia

As I met with my publisher to tell them my story, I came with open hands, offering a book that I didn't *need* to write. If I'd needed to write this book, then it would be a terrible venture. Nobody should write a book with something to prove, begging people to listen to them or believe them. That's entirely too much pressure to put on a reader, and it is way too risky a proposition for a writer. If Jana and I haven't discussed something from every angle, if we haven't agreed that the trauma and triggers and story have been untangled and made whole, then I have no business taking that something to a publisher. I must do the work before it can become my job.

But I also had this idea, this sacred journey out of abuse and into healing, narrated between client and therapist, opening a door of healing to people who have been victims of predators, especially in the church.

Caitlyn has been my editor for many books now, and I want to write all the books with her, for all the reasons. With such tenderness, she listened, and then she said, "Tricia, you keep using the word *victim*, but I think you have the freedom to use the word *survivor*."

Immediately there was a shift within me. Admittedly, I don't love the word *victim*, but I hadn't known there was another word that fit. Of course my editor would find the word I needed.

Jana and I talked about this—how there is a time and a place for both words. Sort of like *wife* and *widow*. Some people suggested I stop using the word *widow* once I married Peter. *Wife* became the greater identity, but *widow* was still tucked deeply inside me. One did not cancel the other.

As I went back and forth between these words, I decided to do some research in my dictionary app, and here's what I found:

victim (noun): "a person harmed, injured, or killed as a result of a crime, accident, or other event or action"; "a person who is tricked or duped"[1]

survivor (noun): "a person who survives, especially a person remaining alive after an event in which others have died"; "a person who copes well with difficulties in their life"; "a person who has experienced abuse or cruel treatment, especially of a sexual or psychological nature"[2]

Interestingly, when I searched for these words in my dictionary app, *survivor* was not included in the free version I had. However, I could upgrade to another version if I paid a few dollars for a yearly subscription. Don't worry, reader. I prevailed. I have many resources when it comes to words and definitions. But the irony was not lost on me.

It costs more to be a survivor than to be a victim.

So I write this to you now as a survivor, counting the cost. Memories are things, *actual things* that live within us. We cannot expect to go back into our memories without paying a cost, be it fatigue, illness, or emotional trauma. The telling requires doing trauma work, releasing the memories that live inside us, so they don't have to have that effect on us. The cost has been great, and not only to me but also to the ones who love me most.

But I also know that healing comes in telling the story a thousand times.

Telling the story afterward can be as traumatic as experiencing it the first time. I often wonder if the trauma is worse when you tell your story but it is disbelieved, distrusted, and used to defame you. Your story needs a safe harbor, in the presence of people who will honor both your vulnerability and your resilience.

Each time you tell your story, something in you heals. There comes a time when you can tell it and it hurts less.

There may even come a time when you hear someone else tell your story because they have woven it into their own. That's when you know you have been a piece of the greatest part of healing. Your healing has helped someone else's.

There are chapters of our lives that we love to live again and again, like returning to a beloved book on a shelf. But there are also chapters we can close when we know how they end. As Brené Brown says, "When we deny our stories, they define us. When we own our stories, we get to write a brave new ending."[3]

May there come a time when your healing has come so far that you can decide that that chapter is finished. (As I finish writing this book, I look forward to the day when I can close the manuscript and let the story be complete.)

When the truth has set you free, you are free indeed.[4] You are free to tell the story to help someone else heal, or—as Jana has taught me—you are free to stop talking about it.

Listening is part of the healing. So, when you listen to someone else's story, you are part of their healing, even if all you do is listen. You don't have to fix anything for them. You don't have to tell them what to do next, you don't have to refer them to a therapist, and you don't have to send groceries to their house. You graciously listen. When you are a safe place for them to tell what has happened, you are part of their healing. People need to be heard.

In the writing workshop that I teach, I coach writers to receive someone else's writing with two simple words: "Thank you." *Thank you for sharing this with me. Your time, your thoughts, your words.* After all, they have just given you a great gift, and you also to them. In listening, you have helped with their own healing, in ways that they don't even know yet.

Now is my chance. Dear reader, thank you.

And if you have read this book and recognized pieces of your own story, either past or present, I want you to hear this: Your instincts are worth listening to. You don't need to be trapped or harmed for a single minute more. You are valuable and loved and worth fighting for.

"Wherever the Spirit of the Lord is, there is freedom."[5] His Spirit is with you. He is beckoning you toward freedom. So break whatever shame and fear is keeping you silenced. Ask for help. Listen to his voice.

When you know that voice instead of agreeing to anything anyone else tells you, you keep your soul alive.[6] And the world needs your soul to be alive, my friend. Come out into the light.

You are safe now.

Jana

In the beginning and in the end, it's still true: If abusers wore name tags to identify themselves, then maybe we would recognize them before they ruin people's lives. But we usually only see them for who they are once the damage is done. So how do we recognize what makes people unsafe, and what do we do about it?

First, learn to recognize the difference between safe people and unsafe people, and trust yourself to recognize the distinction.

Safe people nurture your talents and abilities, helping you become a better version of the person you were created to be. They help you connect with other safe people because love always produces more love. Safe people help mend your wounds. A safe person draws you closer to God and other sources of love, life, energy, and light.

Unsafe people are possessive and controlling, and they fight for the steering wheel. Unsafe people inflict damage on you. They cross boundaries by taking over your property, your body, and your soul. Unsafe people try to acquire other people, to oppress them and own them.

You were not meant to be acquired, oppressed, controlled, or owned *by anyone*.

Gary Thomas writes,

> If someone is getting in the way of you becoming
> the person God created you to be or frustrating the
> work God has called you to do, for you that person
> is toxic. It's not selfish for you to want to be who
> God created you to be, and it's not selfish for you
> to do what God created you to do, so it's important
> to learn how to be on the lookout for toxic people.
> That may mean cutting them out of your life when
> possible or severely limiting your exposure to them
> when there's no better solution.[7]

Nothing is ever all one thing. If a person is unsafe for you, that does not necessarily mean they are a bad person. It means they are unsafe *for you*. Given your individual qualities, tendencies, and patterns, this is not a person you should have in your life. You deserve to be safe in every way, and that is why it is essential to learn to recognize people who are unsafe.

So how do you steer clear of unhealthy people?

Train and sharpen your senses to recognize the distinctions between good and evil, safe and unsafe. Some of us have an intuitive sense of this, and others of us need to identify the clues, look for them, and respond. Most of us are not qualified to professionally diagnose a person with mental-health labels, but we know when we don't feel safe. If your interactions feel toxic, listen to your intuition. You cannot remove unsafe influences until you learn to recognize them.

Tricia needed the help of a third party, both professionally and spiritually. Sometimes you cannot fight off a person who is bigger than you—maybe because they are physically larger or professionally more powerful or maybe because of another power imbalance in play. If you have an addict in your life, you may not be able to handle this boundary on your own, and you may need to seek help from support groups such as Alcoholics Anonymous, Nar-Anon, Alateen, Al-Anon; you may also need to explore legal assistance and/or professional help.

Choosing therapy can feel difficult. You may feel an old stigma surrounding mental health, or you may believe seeking help means that there is something wrong with you. The truth is, to quote my mentor Barb Maiberger,

If you seek out therapy you are a brave person
who is willing to admit that as human beings we
all sometimes need help to navigate in this world

and in our body-mind. Our bodies and our minds are not perfect machines and they don't always feel the way we want them to. *There's nothing shameful about asking for help.* On the contrary, it is a basic human need to know other human beings who can witness our pain and reflect back to us about our problems, joys, and successes.[8]

Above all else, the number one most important and effective way that you can remove unsafe people from your life is by doing this: *Get healthy.* When you are healthy, dangerous people will learn quickly that their dysfunction doesn't work on you. They won't play on your playground because they don't like your top priority: You require safety. Make yourself your own priority.

You may have conceded to someone out of weakness or confusion, as part of a flawed strategy to help you survive, or because they were a con artist who intended from the beginning to steal from you. You may feel like there is nothing you can do to stop the abuse, but that is never the case. You have the agency to pick up the phone and call a counselor. You have the power to write your story. You have the authority to go for a walk, to withdraw and regroup. You have the agency to step back from an invitation and evaluate what lies ahead and who is involved. You don't have to recklessly rush into situations or relationships that may harm you. This path to freedom often requires effort and willingness, and sometimes it requires work. But you are not without power. You are not out of control.

Your offensive strategy may be as basic as this revolutionary tool: Blink, Think, Choice, Voice.[9] People like to believe they would have the courage to resist an order that would cause harm, but research, history, and headlines all show that this is how corrupt leaders make us do things we never intended to. With these four steps, you can blink your eyes, take a second with your thoughts and intuitions, consider your choices, and use your voice. It may sound basic, but that's because our choices can be.

Get yourself safe, and get yourself healthy. That's how you find freedom.

When No Is the Right Answer

Jana

When appropriate, the word *no* is the most powerful two-letter word in the English language. A boundary is not always about building a wall but about drawing a circle around what matters most to you. We don't always need a prison fence with barbed wire because sometimes a white picket fence would do just fine. Sometimes no is the right answer.

When No Is the Right Answer

No is the right answer when saying yes would encourage or enable anything evil.

No is the right answer when our health or well-being is threatened by a controlling or manipulative person.

No is the right answer when we are returning to an old strategy that has never helped in the past.

No is the right answer when we are staying in an unhealthy pattern in order to stay in a relationship.

No is the right answer when we may be jeopardized in any way.

No is the right answer when we are only saying yes to please someone.

When No Is the Wrong Answer

No is the wrong answer when we are avoiding conflict.

No is the wrong answer when it is manipulative, punitive, or simply mean to another person.

No is the wrong answer when we are avoiding an exertion of energy that we can afford.

No is the wrong answer when we are called to be courageous.

Caring for Yourself after Trauma

Jana

As you read this book, you may recognize pieces of your own story, either past or present. I encourage you to consider professional guidance with a licensed mental-health therapist or psychologist, but as you consider exploring this further, these questions and ideas can be a helpful starting point:

1. Stressful, frightening, or distressing events are sometimes traumatic. When we talk about psychological or emotional trauma, we may include situations or events when we felt powerless, afraid, or silenced. When you think of traumas of your life, what comes to mind? Begin to name things that may have been traumatic for you. Remember, no experience is too big or too small to count.

2. As you consider these traumatic experiences, what emotions do you feel? Nothing is ever only one thing. When you have one strong emotion, it's often attached

to other strong emotions. Usually the strongest one is the one we can see and identify, so we grab on to it. But when we identify that strong emotion, as we peel it back, we can reveal other emotions that are quieter and softer. Every person, every emotion, and every experience has layers upon layers. You'll usually not be just sad or just angry.

3. What memories are connected to these emotions? Memories often trigger the brain to experience flashbacks, when we vividly recall a past time or even just the emotions associated with a past event. Do you regularly relive or experience the event? Do you feel afraid again?

4. Do you have a hard time remembering certain features of an event? Sometimes a person may not recall a specific trauma because the memory may have been suppressed or repressed. You may have blocked parts of the trauma that were too overwhelming to process, but in some cases, these blocked memories may resurface through spontaneous recall or guided therapy.

5. Do you avoid certain people, situations, or places? People with PTSD and complex PTSD may experience anxiety, intrusive thoughts, and flashbacks in certain settings. As a result, they may withdraw from others, avoid social situations, and stay away from triggers that could worsen their experience. There is treatment available to manage these symptoms, to support your experience, and to help you create a fulfilling life.

6. Consider the experiences that make you feel powerless. What thoughts come to you when you feel powerless? Where do you sense this feeling in your body? How do you picture it? When you can name those experiences, you can begin to find your power in the face of them.

7. Consider people who are close to you, the traumas they have experienced, and how those traumas may have affected your life. For example, imagine a mother and child walking down a sidewalk, along a line of fenced-in yards. A dog suddenly starts barking on the other side of a fence, and the mother squeezes her child's hand and picks up the pace to quickly get past the barking dog. Even without a bad experience with a dog, the child may learn from this that it's wise to be afraid of dogs. You may not have experienced the bad experience, but you may have been taught to fear the experience because of someone else's trauma.

8. Trauma can hide in different parts of a person's mind and body, affecting their thoughts, emotions, sensations, and behaviors. What are some stories or moments from your life where trauma has been hidden? To find hidden traumas, follow the trail of intense emotions, difficult memories, or even increased heart rate, sweating, or headaches. If you can trace the cause of these, you may find the source of a hidden trauma.

9. What causes you to feel overwhelmed? Instead of rushing past that feeling, pay attention to the moments

or places where you feel overwhelmed. Observe those things in small moments. These may indicate other places where trauma is hiding.

10. Fears are very real, and you can't erase them by denying them. In fact, the opposite may happen: If you avoid or deny your fears, they may affect your marriage, your children, your church, your relationships. Instead of dismissing fears, choose to become aware of them, to ask questions about them. What do you feel afraid of? What might happen if you looked directly at that memory?

11. Isolation can make us feel powerless, and loneliness can magnify difficult emotions and memories. Who can you talk with to begin your healing? You do not have to share your story with a whole group or a room full of people, but perhaps try just one safe person.

12. Even small movements and short exercises can give you a sense of control over your life and your body. Take some slow breaths or go for a walk to remind yourself that you are in charge of your body.

13. Remember that healing is exhausting. There is a very real connection between emotional depletion and physical fatigue. Even when the hard work is mostly the work of your mind, give your body time to rest and recover.

Resources

Anatomy of the Soul: Surprising Connections between Neuro-science and Spiritual Practices That Can Transform Your Life and Relationships by Curt Thompson, MD

The Body Keeps the Score: Brain, Mind, and Body in the Healing of Trauma by Bessel van der Kolk, MD

Boundaries: When to Say Yes, How to Say No to Take Control of Your Life by Dr. Henry Cloud and Dr. John Townsend

Codependent No More: How to Stop Controlling Others and Start Caring for Yourself by Melody Beattie

Combating Cult Mind Control: The #1 Best-Selling Guide to Protection, Rescue, and Recovery from Destructive Cults by Steven Hassan, PhD

EMDR Essentials: A Guide for Clients and Therapists by Barb Maiberger

Healing Trauma: A Pioneering Program for Restoring the Wisdom of Your Body by Peter A. Levine, PhD

Healing the Wounded Heart: The Heartache of Sexual Abuse and the Hope of Transformation by Dan B. Allender

National Survey of Adult Survivors of Sexual Exploitation by Clergy by Baylor University's Diana R. Garland School of Social Work

Sexual Shame in Women and How to Experience Freedom by Joy Skarka

The Sociopath Next Door: The Ruthless versus the Rest of Us by Martha Stout, PhD

Something's Not Right: Decoding the Hidden Tactics of Abuse—and Freeing Yourself from Its Power by Wade Mullen

The Subtle Power of Spiritual Abuse: Recognizing and Escaping Spiritual Manipulation and False Spiritual Authority within the Church by David Johnson and Jeff VanVonderen

Suffering and the Heart of God: How Trauma Destroys and Christ Restores by Diane Langberg, PhD

Take Back Your Life: Recovering from Cults and Abusive Relationships by Janja Lalich and Madeleine Tobias

When Narcissism Comes to Church: Healing Your Community from Emotional and Spiritual Abuse by Chuck DeGroat

Support

for survivors, for those who treat them,
and for those who love them

- » 1in6 (1in6.org)
- » Al-Anon
- » Alateen
- » Alcoholics Anonymous
- » Confusion to Clarity
- » Global Trauma Recovery Institute
- » Nar-Anon
- » National Center for Victims of Crime
- » National Sexual Violence Resource Center
- » National Suicide Prevention Lifeline
- » Rape, Abuse & Incest National Network
- » SESAME: Stop Educator Sexual Abuse, Misconduct & Exploitation

Acknowledgments

Tricia

It has taken me more than a decade to write this book. In that time, a great many people have shown me the slow and steady way of kindness. They have my love and gratitude.

I am deeply grateful to Jana Richardson, Peter Barber, and Cassi Workman. Without you, I would not be healthy.

I want to write all the books with Caitlyn Carlson, who brings out my best work and is gracious with all the rest. I am forever grateful and impressed by the careful hands of Elizabeth Schroll, Olivia Eldredge, David Zimmerman, and Lindsey Bergsma—the Dream Team at NavPress and Tyndale. Thank you to Greg Johnson. Without each of you, I would have no pages.

I am thankful to those who have loved me to fullness and shown me the church at its finest once again. Special gratitude to Cherikay, Joe, Hillary, Bob, Carson, Ruth, Rick, Dan, and every single person who carries the conversations in the Cultivate Community.

I am astounded by the generosity of my earliest readers, who have graciously caught this curveball that was so different from every other story I have told you. Truth has many layers, and you have waited for me to tell them.

And now, my family.

I am forever crazy about my mom and dad, who have walked a thousand days of heartache with each of their children, outnumbered only by ten thousand days of joy and healing. My brother and his wife have held my story from the start. My young men are taller than me, braver than me, and brighter than the sun, moon, and all the stars. My husband, Peter, is my covering, a safe place for me in an unsafe world. Thank you for being able to hold a story like this, a book like this, a wife like me. Without each of you, I would not know myself.

Jana

I would like to thank the many individuals of my therapy practice, with whom I have walked many sacred journeys. I continue to learn from each one of you, which allows me to grow as I continue to help others.

Many helping professionals have reviewed this book in its entirety, throughout its development and publication. Thank you to the following generous experts and peers:

Jayne Statler, MA, LPC, EMDR
Kaci Guilford, MA, LPC, EMDR
Dr. Cassi Workman, MD

Sarah Byram, LPC

Janelle Paris, MAEd, LPCC

Gary Thomas, MA, bestselling author, international
speaker

Zechariah Richardson

Rob Carlson, MA, LPC, EMDR, ACS

Chris Hughes, EdS

Daneille Callow, MA, LPCC

Finally, thank you to my family and friends for all your encouragement and support during this process. With a special thanks to my wonderful husband, the love of my life, who keeps me grounded and supports me in my endeavors, along with my amazing kids, Zechariah and Sydney, the joys of my life, who are always there for me. I love you so much!

Notes

INTRODUCTION | THIS IS HOW IT HAPPENS

1. Joshua Pease, "The Sin of Silence: The Epidemic of Denial about Sexual Abuse in the Evangelical Church," *The Washington Post*, May 31, 2018, https://www.washingtonpost.com/news/posteverything/wp/2018/05/31/feature/the-epidemic-of-denial-about-sexual-abuse-in-the-evangelical-church.

2. "Church Abuse Statistics," Not in Our Church, accessed January 14, 2023, www.notinourchurch.com/statistics.

3. James F. Cobble, Jr., "Screening Children's Workers," *Christianity Today*, summer 2002, https://www.christianitytoday.com/pastors/2002/summer/12.72.html.

4. "Church Abuse Statistics," Not in Our Church.

5. "Church Abuse Statistics," Not in Our Church.

6. "Church Abuse Statistics," Not in Our Church. The website cites this source for this data: Andrew S. Denney, Kent Kerley, Nickolas G. Gross, "Child Sexual Abuse in Protestant Christian Congregations: A Descriptive Analysis of Offense and Offender Characteristics," *Religions* 9, no. 1 (2018), https://doi.org/10.3390/rel9010027. While the study is specific to child sexual abuse, it seems likely that adult sexual abuse by clergy occurs at some of the same locations.

7. "According to this article, there are 2.7 church shootings a year. There are an estimated 378,000 congregations in the United States, which means the likelihood of any congregation being involved in a shooting in any year is approximately one in 126,000." "Church Abuse Statistics," Not in Our Church. The article referenced and quoted by Not in Our Church is: Joe Carter, "How Common Are Church Shootings?" The Gospel Coalition, November 6, 2017, https://www.thegospelcoalition.org/article/common-church-shootings. It's worth noting that the "2.7 church shootings a

year" statistic is based on Carter's review of media reports of shootings within church buildings in the US from 2006 to 2015. The Center for Homicide Research, which compiled a database of shootings anywhere on church property in the US from 1980 to 2005, reported an average of six shootings per year.

8. Martha Stout, *The Sociopath Next Door: The Ruthless versus the Rest of Us* (New York: Broadway Books, 2005), 12.

ONE | THE HOOK

1. Michael J. Fox as Marty McFly, *Back to the Future* (Universal City, CA: Universal Pictures, 1985).
2. Jessica Contrera, "The End of 'Shrink It and Pink It': A History of Advertisers Missing the Mark with Women," *The Washington Post*, June 8, 2016, https://www.washingtonpost.com/lifestyle/style/the-end-of-shrink-it-or-pink-it-a-history-of-advertisers-missing-the-mark-with-women/2016/06/08/3bcb1832-28e9-11e6-ae4a-3cdd5fe74204_story.html.
3. Catherine McNiel, *Long Days of Small Things: Motherhood as a Spiritual Discipline* (Colorado Springs: NavPress, 2017).
4. Emma Dibdin, "6 Podcasts about Cults and Their Enduring Sinister Attraction," *New York Times*, March 20, 2023, https://www.nytimes.com/2023/03/20/arts/podcasts-cults-nxivm-manson.html.
5. Nadia Bolz-Weber, "301. Sarah Edmondson: Actor and Former Member of NXIVM," March 17, 2021, in *The Confessional*, podcast, 30:41, https://nadiabolzweber.com/301-sarah-edmondson.
6. Edward H. Smith, *Confessions of a Confidence Man: A Handbook for Suckers* (New York: Scientific American Publishing, 1923), 279.
7. Bolz-Weber, "301. Sarah Edmondson."

TWO | CHARISMA

1. Wade Mullen, *Something's Not Right: Decoding the Hidden Tactics of Abuse and Freeing Yourself from Its Power* (Carol Stream, IL: Tyndale Momentum, 2020), 57–58.
2. Mike Cosper, "Bonus Episode: A Conversation with Tim Keller," *The Rise and Fall of Mars Hill* (podcast), July 1, 2022, https://www.christianitytoday.com/ct/podcasts/rise-and-fall-of-mars-hill/tim-keller-mike-cosper-mars-hill-bonus.html. "The other thing that I notice, and nobody talks about it anymore the way they used to, is the mistaking of gifts for grace. . . . And so what's going on in a lot of these megachurches, frankly—in fact, everywhere—is what everybody's concentrating on is really not the character of the leaders but the talent."
3. Tim Keller in Cosper, "Bonus Episode."
4. "Have You Confidence in Me to Trust Me with Your Watch until

Tomorrow?" Isegoria.net, July 7, 2019, https://www.isegoria.net/2019/07/have-you-confidence-in-me-to-trust-me-with-your-watch-until-tomorrow. "1889's 'Con Man' a Short Form of 1849's 'Confidence Man,'" *Deseret News*, October 20, 1996, https://www.deseret.com/1996/10/20/19272696/1889-s-con-man-a-short-form-of-1849-s-confidence-man.

5. Martha Stout, *Outsmarting the Sociopath Next Door: How to Protect Yourself against a Ruthless Manipulator* (New York: Harmony Books, 2020), 25.

6. Raven Ishak, "8 Signs Your Relationship Is Really Just a String of Manipulative Love Bombs," Well + Good, updated January 24, 2023, https://www.wellandgood.com/love-bomb.

7. *Merriam-Webster*, s.v. "thrall (*n.*)," accessed February 24, 2023, https://www.merriam-webster.com/dictionary/thrall.

8. *Merriam-Webster*, s.v. "thrall (*n.*)."

9. *Merriam-Webster*, s.v. "enthrall (*v.*)," accessed February 24, 2023, https://www.merriam-webster.com/dictionary/enthrall.

10. Janja Lalich and Madeleine Tobias, *Take Back Your Life: Recovering from Cults and Abusive Relationships*, 2nd ed. (Berkeley, CA: Bay Tree, 2006), chap. 1.

11. Mullen, *Something's Not Right*, 34–35.

THREE | MANIPULATION

1. *Merriam-Webster*, s.v. "manipulate (*v.*)," accessed June 1, 2023, https://www.merriam-webster.com/dictionary/manipulate.

2. *Merriam-Webster*, s.v. "manipulate (*v.*)."

3. Janja Lalich and Madeleine Tobias, *Take Back Your Life: Recovering from Cults and Abusive Relationships*, 2nd ed. (Berkeley, CA: Bay Tree, 2006), chap. 3.

4. Seth Godin, *The Practice: Shipping Creative Work* (New York: Portfolio, 2020), 46.

FOUR | SECRETS

1. C. S. Lewis, *The Four Loves* (New York: Harcourt, Brace & World, 1960), 169.

2. Galatians 5:6, author's paraphrase.

3. Ann Voskamp (@AnnVoskamp), "'You think evil . . .'—Joseph Brodsky, exiled Russian poet" Twitter, January 13, 2018, 8:56 p.m., https://twitter.com/AnnVoskamp/status/952388906758131718. Marie Howe, a student of Brodsky, shared this quote in an On Being conversation: https://onbeing.org/programs/marie-howe-the-power-of-words-to-save-us-may2017.

4. The Collected Works of C. G. Jung, Vol. 16, *Practice of Psychotherapy: Essays on the Psychology of the Transference and Other Subjects*, 2nd ed., trans. R. F. C. Hull (Princeton, NJ: Princeton University Press, 1985), 55.

5. Mullen credits Erving Goffman for identifying these types of secrets in *The Presentation of Self in Everyday Life* (Edinburgh: University of Edinburgh, 1956). Wade Mullen, *Something's Not Right: Decoding the Hidden Tactics of Abuse and Freeing Yourself from Its Power* (Carol Stream, IL: Tyndale Momentum, 2020), 18–23.
6. Mullen, *Something's Not Right*, 18.
7. Mullen, *Something's Not Right*, 17.
8. Diane Langberg, *Suffering and the Heart of God: How Trauma Destroys and Christ Restores* (Greensboro, NC: New Growth Press, 2015), 223.

FIVE | TRAUMA

1. Dwight Garner, "A Gifted Writer Returns with a Supremely Harrowing Novel," review of *Dear Miss Metropolitan: A Novel*, by Carolyn Ferrell, *New York Times*, July 5, 2021, Book Review, https://www.nytimes.com/2021/07/05/books/review-dear-miss-metropolitan-carolyn-ferrell.html.
2. "Object in motion . . .": Newton's first law. For more on bodies getting stuck in trauma, see Bessel van der Kolk, *The Body Keeps the Score: Brain, Mind, and Body in the Healing of Trauma* (New York: Penguin Books, 2015).
3. "PTSD: National Center for PTSD," US Department of Veterans Affairs, accessed May 1, 2023, https://www.ptsd.va.gov/understand/common/common_adults.asp.
4. "Complex Trauma Disorder," Center for Treatment of Anxiety and Mood Disorders, accessed May 1, 2023, https://www.centerforanxietydisorders.com/complex-trauma-disorder.
5. Pedram Shojai, *The Urban Monk: Eastern Wisdom and Modern Hacks to Stop Time and Find Success, Happiness, and Peace* (New York: Rodale, 2016), 4.
6. For a brief overview of these changes, see Emma Cameron, "Trauma Therapy Has Changed—Here's How," emmacameron.com, September 5, 2020, https://emmacameron.com/trauma/trauma-therapy-has-changed-heres-how.

SIX | UNTANGLING SHAME

1. Joy Skarka, *Sexual Shame in Women and How to Experience Freedom* (Eugene, OR: Wipf & Stock, 2022).
2. Skarka, *Sexual Shame in Women*, xii.
3. Timothy Keller, "The Silent Sovereignty of God," sermon given July 22, 2022, https://podcast.gospelinlife.com/e/the-silent-sovereignty-of-god.
4. As quoted in Bessel van der Kolk, *The Body Keeps the Score: Brain, Mind, and Body in the Healing of Trauma* (New York: Penguin Books, 2015), 127. He calls this *Auden's rule* because it's from a poem by W. H. Auden.

5. For a brief overview of the cycle of abuse, see https://www.verywellhealth .com/cycle-of-abuse-5210940.

6. Nicole McDermott, "Trauma Bonding: What You Need to Know—and How to Get Help," Forbes, updated March 31, 2023, https://www.forbes .com/health/mind/what-is-trauma-bonding.

EIGHT | WALKING AWAY

1. Genesis 7:16.

2. Genesis 3:23.

3. Deuteronomy 32:51-52.

4. Matthew 10:14, NIV.

5. Gary Thomas, *When to Walk Away: Finding Freedom from Toxic People* (Grand Rapids, MI: Zondervan, 2019), 17.

6. Thomas, *When to Walk Away*, 227. Thomas lists these instances in his appendix "Jesus Walking Away."

7. Thomas, *When to Walk Away*, 30.

8. Cynthia Vinney, "The Marshmallow Test: Delayed Gratification in Children," ThoughtCo., updated July 31, 2019, https://www.thoughtco .com/the-marshmallow-test-4707284.

9. Alix Spiegel and Lulu Miller, "The Personality Myth," June 24, 2016, in *Invisibilia* (podcast), https://www.npr.org/2016/06/24/482837932/read -the-transcript.

10. Spiegel and Miller, "The Personality Myth."

11. Matthew 19:26, NIV.

12. Ezekiel 36:26.

13. 2 Timothy 2:25-26.

NINE | GRIEVING

1. Gary Thomas, *When to Walk Away: Finding Freedom from Toxic People* (Grand Rapids, MI: Zondervan, 2019), 159–60.

2. Brené Brown, *Atlas of the Heart: Mapping Meaningful Connection and the Language of Human Experience* (New York: Random House, 2021), xviii–xix.

TEN | NAMING WHAT HAPPENED

1. Madeleine L'Engle, *Walking on Water: Reflections on Faith and Art* (New York: Convergent Books, 2016), 140.

2. Tristine Rainer, *Your Life as Story: Discovering the "New Autobiography" and Writing Memoir as Literature* (New York: Jeremy P. Tarcher/Putnam, 1998), 39.

3. Diane Langberg, *Suffering and the Heart of God: How Trauma Destroys and Christ Restores* (Greensboro, NC: New Growth Press, 2015), 224.

4. Curt Thompson and Pepper Sweeney, "Trauma: Creating Beauty in the Bomb Craters of Our Lives," March 1, 2022, in *Being Known Podcast*, https://podcasts.apple.com/us/podcast/s4e1-trauma-creating-beauty-in-the-bomb-craters-of-our-lives/id1556261828?i=1000552593298.

5. Thompson and Sweeney, "Trauma: Creating Beauty."

6. Ann Voskamp, *The Way of Abundance: A 60-Day Journey into a Deeply Meaningful Life* (Grand Rapids, MI: Zondervan, 2018), 94.

7. Curt Thompson and Pepper Sweeney, "Trauma and the Brain: It's Not What You Think," March 23, 2022, in *Being Known Podcast*, https://podcasts.apple.com/us/podcast/s4e4-trauma-and-the-brain-its-not-what-you-think/id1556261828?i=1000554975412.

8. Thompson and Sweeney, "Trauma and the Brain."

ELEVEN | HEALING BODY, MIND, AND HEART

1. Bessel van der Kolk, *The Body Keeps the Score: Brain, Mind, and Body in the Healing of Trauma* (New York: Penguin Books, 2015), 317.

2. Licia Sky, quoted in van der Kolk, *The Body Keeps the Score*, 318–19.

3. Van der Kolk, *The Body Keeps the Score*, chap. 3.

4. Van der Kolk, *The Body Keeps the Score*, 80.

5. Van der Kolk, *The Body Keeps the Score*, 45.

6. Cheryl Strayed, *Brave Enough* (New York: Alfred A. Knopf, 2015), 10.

7. Barb Maiberger, *EMDR Essentials: A Guide for Clients and Therapists* (New York: W. W. Norton & Company, 2009), 8.

8. Jeremiah 6:14, TLB.

TWELVE | FORGIVING

1. Janja Lalich and Madeleine Tobias, *Take Back Your Life: Recovering from Cults and Abusive Relationships*, 2nd ed. (Berkeley, CA: Bay Tree, 2006), chap. 9.

2. John Eldredge, *Wild at Heart: Discovering the Secret of a Man's Soul*, expanded ed. (Nashville: Thomas Nelson, 2021), 119.

3. Kelly Corrigan, "Three Stories of Extraordinary Forgiveness with Wanda Holland Greene," November 23, 2020, in *Kelly Corrigan Wonders* (podcast), https://www.kellycorrigan.com/kelly-corrigan-wonders/wanda4.

4. Angelou shared this wisdom in an interview with Oprah: "Oprah Winfrey: Forgiveness," January 13, 2021, in *Super Soul* (podcast), https://www.oprah.com/own-podcasts/oprah-winfrey-forgiveness.

5. Angelou also shared this wisdom in an interview with Oprah: "Super Soul Special: Dr. Maya Angelou, Part 1: 9 Words That Changed Her Life," March 29, 2023, in *Super Soul* (podcast), https://www.oprah.com/own-podcasts/super-soul-special-dr-maya-angelou-part-1-9-words-that-changed-her-life.

6. Brené Brown, "Spirituality, Certitude, and Infinite Love, Part 1 of 2, with Father Richard Rohr," April 20, 2022, in *Unlocking Us Podcast*, https://brenebrown.com/podcast/spirituality-certitude-and-infinite -love-part-1-of-2.

EPILOGUE | BECOMING FREE

1. *Oxford Dictionary*, iPhone ed., v. 15.7.471 (Oxford Languages, 2023), s.v. "victim (*n.*)."
2. *Oxford Dictionary*, iPhone ed., v. 15.7.471 (Oxford Languages, 2023), s.v. "survivor (*n.*)."
3. Brené Brown, "Own Our History. Change the Story.," brenebrown.com, June 18, 2015, https://brenebrown.com/articles/2015/06/18/own-our -history-change-the-story.
4. John 8:32.
5. 2 Corinthians 3:17.
6. Robert Louis Stevenson: "To know what you prefer, instead of humbly saying Amen to what the world tells you you ought to prefer, is to have kept your soul alive." "An Inland Voyage" in *The Works of Robert Louis Stevenson*, vol. I (New York: Charles Scribner's Sons, 1925), 15.
7. Gary Thomas, *When to Walk Away: Finding Freedom from Toxic People* (Grand Rapids, MI: Zondervan, 2019), 13.
8. Barb Maiberger, *EMDR Essentials: A Guide for Clients and Therapists* (New York: W. W. Norton & Company, 2009), 14. Emphasis added.
9. "Blink. Think. Choice. Voice.," accessed March 15, 2023, blinkthinkchoicevoice.com, based on the book *Intelligent Disobedience* by Ira Chaleff.

NavPress is the book-publishing arm of The Navigators.

Since 1933, The Navigators has helped people around the world bring hope and purpose to others in college campuses, local churches, workplaces, neighborhoods, and hard-to-reach places all over the world, face-to-face and person-by-person in an approach we call Life-to-Life® discipleship. We have committed together to know Christ, make Him known, and help others do the same.®

Would you like to join this adventure of discipleship and disciplemaking?

- Take a Digital Discipleship Journey at **navigators.org/disciplemaking**.
- Get more discipleship and disciplemaking content at **thedisciplemaker.org**.
- Find your next book, Bible, or discipleship resource at **navpress.com**.

@NavPressPublishing

@NavPress

@navpressbooks